THE CAMPUS GUIDE

University of Virginia

THE CAMPUS GUIDE

University of Virginia

Richard Guy Wilson and Sara A. Butler

Photographs by Walter Smalling Jr.

Princeton Architectural Press

NEW YORK | *1999*

To Kristina F. Wilson
and Sara Spence Butler

Princeton Architectural Press
37 East 7th Street
New York, NY 10003
212.995.9620

For a free catalog of other books published by Princeton Architectural Press,
call toll free 1.800.722.6657 or visit our web site at www.papress.com

Editing: Jan Cigliano
Design: Sara E. Stemen and Brian Noyes
Maps: Jane Garvie
Special thanks to Eugenia Bell, Caroline Green, Clare Jacobson, Therese Kelly,
Mark Lamster, and Anne Nitschke of Princeton Architectural Press
—Kevin C. Lippert, publisher

Library of Congress Cataloging-in-Publication Data
Wilson, Richard Guy, 1940–
        The campus guide: University of Virginia / Richard Guy Wilson and
Sara A. Butler ; photographs by Walter Smalling Jr.
            p. cm.
        Includes bibliographical references (p. 146) and index.
        ISBN 1-56898-168-6   (alk. paper)
    1. University of Virginia—Guidebooks. 2. University of Virginia—
Buildings—Guidebooks.   I. Butler, Sara A., 1952– . II. Title.
III. Title: University of Virgina.
LD5679.W55 1998
378.755'481—dc21   98-53081
                                                                         CIP

03 02 01 00 99   5 4 3 2 1   First Edition

Acknowledgments

This work has been a collaborative effort. Richard Guy Wilson was primarily responsible for the Introduction and Walk 1. Sara Butler prepared Walks 2 through 7. Mary V. Hughes, University Landscape Architect, contributed the garden entries to Walk 1. Generous support for this project has been provided by the Samuel A. Anderson III, Office of the Architect for the University of Virginia, and by John T. Casteen III, President of the University of Virginia. We also gratefully acknowledge the assistance of the following individuals: Michael Plunkett and the staff of the Special Collections Department at the University of Virginia Library, Marsha Trimble, Curator of Special Collections at the University of Virginia Law Library, and Garth Anderson and Jeffrey Tilman of Facilities Management. Over the years, many historians, faculty, and students have studied the architecture of the University of Virginia. Some of these are noted in the bibliography. We owe a special debt to several historians, including C. Allan Brown and Marie Frank; members of the faculty, especially James Murray Howard and K. Edward Lay; as well as numerous students who have contributed research, including Marie Castro, Laurel Haarlow, John-Lee Holmes, Elizabeth Hughes, Adrienne Lakadat, Joseph Lasala, Scott Meacham, Elizabeth Byrd Oliver, Denis McNamara, Charles Rosenblum, Patricia Sherwood, Jennifer Steen, and Catherine Zipf. We are indebted to Jan Cigliano for her careful editing of the text and Walter Smalling for his fine photography. Finally, we thank Betty Leake, secretary in the Department of Architectural History for her ongoing support.

How to use this book

This guide is intended for visitors, alumni, and students who wish to have an insider's look at the most historic and interesting buildings on campus and around town, from Thomas Jefferson's Rotunda and The Lawn, to Michael Graves's Bryan Hall and Tod Williams's and Billie Tsein's Hereford College.

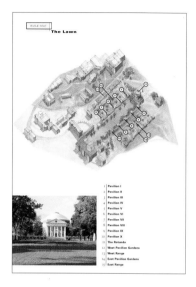

The book is divided into seven Walks covering the major areas of the campus. Each Walk, or chapter, comprises an introductory section that describes the history of the area, with a map and a list of the buildings, followed by entries on each building (or cluster of buildings). The entries are accompanied by a photograph of the site and historical and architectural information telling the reader about the building's defining characteristics.

Campus buildings open: 9am–5pm Monday–Friday, year-round.
Gardens open: dawn–dusk daily, year-round.
Rotunda tours: 10am–4pm Monday–Friday; 12noon–5pm Saturday;
    closed holidays, year-round. Admission: free.
Admissions tours: 11am–2pm Monday–Friday; 11am Saturday, year-round.
Alderman Library open: 8am–10pm Monday–Friday; 9am–8pm Saturday;
    11am–10pm Sunday, September–May.
University of Virginia Bookstore open: 8:30am–7:00pm Monday–Friday;
    10am–6pm Saturday; 11am–6pm Sunday.

Further information from:

    University of Virginia Visitors Center
    Ivy Road/Route 250 Business East
    Charlottesville 22903
    804.924.0311
    www.virginia.edu

Foreword

Every May, soon-to-be graduates and their families and friends gather on the Lawn at the University of Virginia for Final Exercises of the academic year. It is a colorful ceremony, filled with pomp and tradition but lightened by the festivity and promise of the day. Proceeding from the Rotunda at the Lawns north end, students take a symbolic walk from the past to the future. Surrounding them is the Academical Village, Thomas Jefferson's architectural legacy that stands today not as a fragile relic of the past but as

the vibrant centerpiece of a modern university. By his own account, Jefferson was the father of the University of Virginia.

No other university has such a relationship with its founder. He conceived the University when there was no similar institution, wrote the curriculum, convened the faculty, devised standards for admission of students and rules for student behavior, and wrote statements of purpose and mission that endure to this day. Moreover, he acquired the land, raised the money, and designed and supervised the construction of the original buildings, which remain even now the intellectual and spiritual core of the community.

The Academical Village is the physical embodiment of Jefferson's ideals. He intended the Rotunda to house not a chapel but a library. As he planned, students and faculty members still live side by side in the rooms and pavilions lining the Lawn. Freedom and self-governance characterized life of the early institution, and those ideals remain woven into the fabric of the University today.

Those of us who live and work in view of Jefferson's architectural legacy experience it in public and private dimensions. Grand events like Final Exercises are matched in meaning and power by moments as simple as a twilight walk on the Lawn. It is here we feel the strength and vision of a single individual who pursued his dream, one visible not only in its architecture but also in its dedication to education as the cornerstone of democracy. As keepers of that dream, we take great pride in helping it continue to unfold.

John T. Casteen III
President
The University of Virginia

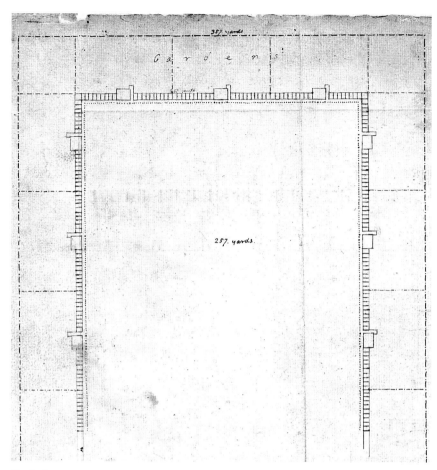

Preliminary ground plan, August 1814, Thomas Jefferson

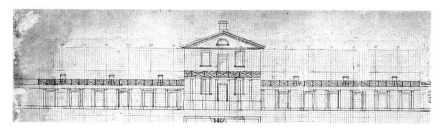

Elevation, showing typical pavilion and dormitories, August 1814, Thomas Jefferson

Sketch for elevation, Benjamin Henry Latrobe, letter to Thomas Jefferson, July 24, 1817

Introduction to the University of Virginia

The experience of setting foot on the Lawn at the University of Virginia can scarcely be communicated; the intensity of Thomas Jefferson's vision and accomplishment takes away one's breath. A green plain of gently stepped terraces lies underneath, the sky arches out overhead, and red brick buildings fronted by white columns of different sizes and shapes roll out, merging together in the distance. Amorphous and spidery webs of ash trees offset the regularity of the colonnades' march. The Rotunda, a large cylindrical and domed structure, anchors one end of the Lawn while a series of taller buildings, the pavilions, rises up from the milk-bottle-shaped colonnades. Up close, acanthus leaves, volutes, swags, dentils, moldings, ox skulls, putti, cross-hatched balconies, and balustrades compete for one's attention. The other end of the Lawn holds more columnar structures. Interspersed along the covered walkways behind the Lawn's colonnades, the openings provide vistas and lead the visitor along serpentine walls. At the end, arcades link two more rows of buildings. Beyond lies more of the university designed by McKim, Mead & White, Fiske Kimball, Pietro Belluschi, Michael Graves, Tod Williams and Billie Tsein, and many more. Some of these buildings continue Jefferson's building palette of red brick and white stone or wood trim, but also appearing are more modern steel, aluminum, and concrete material. All of these buildings and spaces speak of different efforts, ideals, and possibilities.

The University of Virginia is widely acknowledged as one of America's great educational institutions. That reputation rests upon its academic accomplishments and architecture, particularly the "Academical Village," or the Lawn, a creation of its founder, Thomas Jefferson. The Lawn is world famous, with tens of thousands of visitors every year, and it is constantly cited as one of the great American architectural achievements. The Lawn is both a ubiquitous symbol of learning and an example of a harmonious environment. The university, or in the local colloquialism, "the Grounds," as with most American campuses created prior to 1945, is utopian, a world apart, or a "city upon the hill" in which great ideas would be conceived and transmitted to succeeding generations. Although in many ways this is still true, what began as a small institution for several hundred young men, with eight faculty and a few staff on 196 acres, now has an enrollment of more than 18,000 female and male students, more than 3,200 faculty, and 7,700 staff, and sprawls across 1,065 acres.

The university's architecture represents a dialogue between buildings and individuals. In some cases the conversation engages Jefferson's vision, or as it is sometimes described, his "lengthened shadow," and how succeeding generations modified his concept. At other times, Jefferson appears to have left the room, and a different voice expresses its vision. These

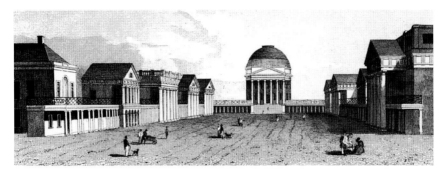

University of Virginia, Charlottesville, 1831, William Goodacre, draughtsman; Fenner Sears & Co, engraver; H. L. Hinton & Simpkin and Marshall, publisher

competing voices are, of course, part of the nature of the modern American university. What is different at the University of Virginia is the strength of that original vision and its enduring influence. The university exudes a palpable sense of time that can be both a hindrance and a reassurance.

The architecture of the University's campus—meaning not just buildings but the entire ensemble of topography, space, and landscape—developed into far more than Jefferson ever could have envisioned. This change epitomizes the history of other American universities and colleges as they have responded to population growth and new ideas about the nature of higher education. And the architecture has changed as well; new curricula demand different buildings, as do new ideas about form and style. The development has five periods: Neoclassical Academical Village (1779–c. 1826), Romantic Picturesque Village (c. 1826–c. 1893), University Beautiful (c. 1893–c. 1950), Campus Suburban (c. 1950–c. 1976), and presently, University Neotraditional (c. 1976–today). Each is distinct with its own attitudes, buildings, and spaces.

Neoclassical Academical Village (1779–c. 1826)

Thomas Jefferson explained to George Washington in 1786: "Liberty can never be safe but in the hands of the people themselves, and that, too, of the people with a certain degree of instruction."[1] The University of Virginia is a product of this belief and of the Enlightenment and the Age of Reason. Jefferson, in company with many of his contemporaries in the United States and Europe, believed that the power of the human mind and reason could make the world understandable. The rule of balance, proportion, and equal measure created a knowable universe. Jefferson was perhaps the foremost American representative of this age, and attempted through his houses, Monticello and Poplar Forest, to demonstrate rationality and high culture. Jefferson's concept of government was essentially Lockean, a social contract

1   Thomas Jefferson to George Washington, January 4, 1786, in *The Papers of Thomas Jefferson*, ed. Julian P. Boyd (Princeton: Princeton University Press, 1950), vol. 9, 151.

that depended not on wise rulers but an informed citizenry. Education, Jefferson believed, advances "the prosperity, the power, and the happiness of a nation," but also education had a political aim.[2] William Thornton, the architect of the United States Capitol in Washington, DC, observed on learning of Jefferson's attempt to create the University of Virginia: "It gives me great pleasure to find Virginia disposed to erect an extensive College which must produce great effects by Example. I was also pleased to see an Acct. of the meeting of such distinguished Characters as the three Presidents [Jefferson, Madison, Monroe] of the United States on so praiseworthy an Occasion. How different to the meeting of the three Emperors on the Continent of Europe, after a bloody battle."[3] Thornton perceived right at the beginning that a political dimension underlay Jefferson's efforts to establish a university.

During his term as governor of Virginia, Jefferson announced *A Bill for the Modern General Diffusion of Knowledge* in 1779. Written during the Revolutionary War, Jefferson far in advance of his contemporaries envisioned the state assuming the responsibility of educating the populace. He promoted a three-tier system: a primary level open to all "free" children; a collegiate level for the teaching of Latin, Greek, and higher mathematics; and, at the apex, a state-supported university devoted to specialized knowledge. Although he failed in getting the legislation passed, he returned to this concept many times in succeeding years, both for the Commonwealth of Virginia and at the national level. Early in 1800, Jefferson explained to Dr. Joseph Priestley: "We wish to establish in the upper country [of Virginia] and more centrally for the State, a University on a plan so broad and liberal and modern, as to be worth patronizing with the public support, and be a temptation to the youth of other States to come and drink of the cup of knowledge and fraternize with us."[4]

So well known was his interest in higher education that officials from other states would approach him for advice. Jefferson's response went beyond just platitudes to the concrete as he wrote in 1805: "The greatest danger will be over-building themselves, by attempting a large house in the beginning, sufficient to contain the whole institution. Large houses are always ugly, inconvenient, exposed to the accident of fire, and bad in cases of infection. A plain small house for the school and lodging of each professor is best. These connected by covered ways out of which the rooms of the students should open would be best. These may be built only as they shall be wanting. In fact a university should not be a house, but a village."[5] In embryo Jefferson had envisioned what would be the design of the University of Virginia.

---

2   Jefferson from second draft of Rockfish Gap Commission, quoted in Dumas Malone, *Jefferson and His Time*, vol. 6, *The Sage of Monticello* (Boston: Little Brown, 1981), 276.
3   Thornton to Jefferson, May 27, 1817, Library of Congress.
4   Jefferson to Dr. Joseph Priestley, Jan. 18, 1800, in *The Writings of Thomas Jefferson*, ed. Paul I. Ford (New York: Putman and Sons, 1892–1899), vol. 7, 407–09.
5   Jefferson to L. W. Tazewell, January 5, 1805, Special Collections, University of Virginia.

After many years, or as Jefferson described, "It is a bantling of forty years' birth and nursing," the University of Virginia came into existence between 1814 and 1826.[6] In 1814, a nephew, Peter Carr, approached Jefferson concerning the establishment of an Albemarle Academy. Jefferson, as was his wont, took control of the proposal, produced an initial plan (shown on page 2) and renamed it "Central College." The proposal went to the state legislature, where after the usual delays, it passed. In 1816, Governor Wilson Cary Nicholas appointed to the first Board of Visitors Jefferson, James Monroe, James Madison, John Hartwell Cocke, and Joseph Carrington Cabell. The first board meeting took place in May 1817, and to no one's surprise, the board selected Jefferson as rector (or chief executive). Already a name change was in front of the legislature, but not until January 1819 did Central College become the University of Virginia. Already in April 1817 Jefferson had inspected and purchased from John Perry a farm once owned by President James Monroe. Described as a "poor old turned out field," it was on a ridge about one mile west of the small village of Charlottesville. The site needed to be leveled, materials purchased or manufactured, construction started, and the design refined beyond the two rough sketches Jefferson had drawn up for the Albemarle Academy in 1814. By July 19, 1817, Jefferson could report: "Our squares are laid off, the brickyard begun, and the leveling will be begun in the course of the week."[7] The cornerstone ceremony occurred on October 6, 1817, and for the next nine years, until 1826, one of the largest construction projects yet undertaken in the United States came about outside the small town of Charlottesville.

The university that Jefferson designed and helped build was a rationalist neoclassical enterprise in both form and spirit. Jefferson wrote in 1820 when the construction had advanced: "This institution will be based on the illimitable freedom of the human mind. For here we are not afraid to follow truth wherever it may lead, nor to tolerate any error so long as reason is left free to combat it."[8] Jefferson drew up a unique curriculum, in reality a postgraduate school, in which the student would arrive with a collegiate degree and specialize; his diplomas were of two grades: doctor and graduate. Jefferson selected the books for the library and drew up a list of 6,800 volumes. For the study of law and government, Jefferson recommended Locke's *Second Treatise*, Sidney's *Discourses*, the Federalist papers, the Declaration of Independence, Madison's Virginia Resolution of 1798, and Washington's "Farewell Address."[9] He expressed antipathy to Plato's works as antiliberty.

6   Jefferson to Cabell, Dec. 18, 1817, quoted in Malone, *Sage of Monticello*, 270.
7   Jefferson to Cocke, July 19, 1817, Jefferson Papers, Library of Congress.
8   Jefferson to William Roscoe, Dec. 27, 1820, in *The Writings of Thomas Jefferson*, eds. A. A. Liscomb and A. E. Bergh (Washington, DC: Thomas Jefferson Memorial Foundation, 1903) vol. XV, 303.
9   *Jefferson's Ideas on a University Library: Letters from the Founder of the University of Virginia to a Boston Bookseller*, ed. Elizabeth Cometti (Charlottesville: Tracy W. McGregor Library, 1950); and, *1828 Catalogue of the Library of the University of Virginia*, ed. William H. Peden, "University of Virginia Bibliographical Series" (Charlottesville: Alderman Library of the University of Virginia, 1945), 6.

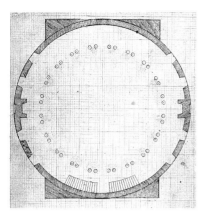

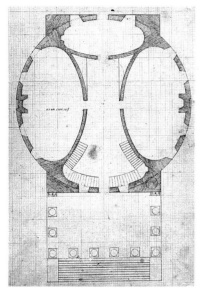

Rotunda, first floor plan; plan of dome room, 1818–1819, Thomas Jefferson

As an institution of the Enlightenment the university was nonsectarian: no religious body dominated it, in contrast to other American colleges and universities. Even state-supported schools such as the Universities of North Carolina and South Carolina, which preceded the University of Virginia, had chapels and were controlled by religious groups. Jefferson was not antireligion, or anti-Christian, but he was a deist and believed that Jesus of Nazareth was a great moral philosopher, not a divine person. He also believed in freedom of religion and not state-supported, or mandated, religious practices. Jefferson's rejection of the special status of religion meant not a chapel as the central structure but a library. He did not forbid religious services on the grounds and they took place, but he hoped that seminaries would be established in the neighborhood, similar to Oxford or Cambridge. Instead of men of the cloth—as were practically all higher-education instructors up to the 1870s—Jefferson sought recognized specialists. Hence, through an agent he hired five English, Scottish, and German professors who were not clerics.

The University's plan and form was neoclassical. Although scholars have had a field day in claiming various prototypes for the university's plan, there is no one ultimate source. Its order makes it unique in comparison with the rather random assemblage at other American universities. In a sense, Jefferson applied European neoclassical urban design principles that were in general ignored in the spatially amorphous America. Many of the specific forms and details at the University are Renaissance and ultimately Roman in source, but to focus exclusively on them is to miss the larger import. Jefferson provided a new model for the American university, neoclassical in form, enlightenment in spirit: nature in the village, the village in the countryside.

Romantic Picturesque Village (c. 1826–c. 1893)

The problem of how to add to the finite form of the Academical Village, especially with a picturesque vocabulary, dominates the University for the next sixty years. Jefferson's ideals of form and spirit confront reality, and inevitably, with growth and changes in interests and curricula, the Academical Village becomes something different.

The romantic spirit, which seeks intensity of emotion rather than reason, can be seen with the first group of students. Edgar Allan Poe entered in January 1826, excelled in Latin and French, and moved into a room on West Range (assumed to be no. 13), which already had the name of "Rowdy Row," and experimented with homemade peach brandy. Jefferson would not have approved. Poe left the University without a degree, but while there he wrote the poem "Tamerlane," and his stories "William Wilson" (1839) and "A Tale of the Ragged Mountains" (1844) reflect his life there. His poem "To Helen" (1823, 1831, 1845), with the lines: "To the glory that was Greece / And the grandeur that was Rome," may refer to the Lawn. A fellow student of Poe's wrote later in 1826: "The number of students that have matriculated is 180 [sic, records indicate 177], 12 of them have been expelled and suspended."

Prior to his death, Jefferson discovered that his ideal student was in short supply, for instead of education many of the students' interests ran to drinking, brawling, gambling, and dueling. Many carried firearms. Periodic student riots broke out, and the murder of Professor John A. G. Davis during a revel on the Lawn in 1840 ultimately led to the famous honor code. Most of the students who came to the University were not prepared

"View of the University of Virginia, Charlottesville & Monticello, Taken From Lewis Mountain, 1856," Edward Sachse, draughtsman; Casamir Bohn, publisher

academically, and very shortly after Jefferson's death the curriculum was modified to follow the more traditional classical format of other universities, and the Bachelor of Arts degree instituted. Instead of postgraduate specialization, students took a standardized curriculum.

The number of students varies widely: not until 1834 are more than 200 in residence; in the 1850s it grows to over 600 students; falls to a low of 54 in 1864 during the Civil War; recovers to 490 in 1866, and stays in that range until the later 1890s when it once again reaches 600. Jefferson's plan provided 108 student rooms (today 107), which until the 1960s frequently had two students to a room. The remainder lived in boardinghouses scattered around the area such as on Carr's Hill, the Corner, and in a few University-sponsored residences such as Monroe Hill House. How to house students beyond the Lawn emerges as one of the problems that continue to vex the University.

Jefferson's neoclassical village contained elements that might be considered picturesque. Placed in the middle of farmland on a hilltop, it gave the impression of a large garden folly, as early views such as the Sachse-Bohn print of 1856 indicate. He adjusted the form to the landscape and selected—if he did not actually plant—the grass and trees on the Lawn itself. The central Lawn, with its seeming order and balance, actually was asymmetrical with the different fronts of the pavilions on each side. Just prior to his death in 1826, Jefferson designed the Anatomical Theater. Professor Dunglison had complained about cutting up cadavers in Pavilion X, and Jefferson responded with an amphitheater of tiered seats within a low, square structure. He located it across from Hotel A, creating, as he said, the beginning of a new street. (Torn down in 1939, the Anatomical Theater stood in front of Alderman Library.) Already the unity of the Lawn was compromised.

In a similar way, over the next sixty years spaces around the original Lawn were appropriated for new buildings and other uses. The professors' garden tracts and sheds spotted the University's property. Outhouses, sheds, and other structures sprang up within the pavilion gardens and along the walks behind the ranges. The need for a large public hall and more classroom space led the University to commission Robert Mills in 1851 to design an Annex to the Rotunda. Mills seemed a logical choice; he studied with Jefferson in 1803, and subsequently achieved renown for his severe neoclassic edifices. Mills's addition fulfilled its purpose with a hall seating 1,200 (and where a reproduction of Raphael's *School of Athens* hung), but the exterior suited nobody; its gargantuan proportions overwhelmed the Rotunda. From a distance the Rotunda lost its distinctive shape and looked like a giant pollywog devouring its smaller siblings, the pavilions and dormitories of the Lawn.

The picturesque aesthetic calls for variety, and increasingly each building asserted itself, separate from the Academical Village. In 1856 the University Board of Visitors decided to engage a landscape gardener and architect. In 1858 William Abbot Pratt took the position as "superintendent of buildings and grounds." Already, Pratt had designed a Gothic-inspired

Rotunda Annex, 1851–1853, Robert Mills

Gatehouse (1856) and he produced a plan that thoroughly romanticized the grounds with curving walks, clumps of trees, and other picturesque features.

Pratt's most notable design was a chapel to be placed at the end of the Lawn, opposite the Rotunda. The reputation as a heathen institution had continued; in 1829 Episcopal Bishop William Mead predicted the University's "destruction" when he preached that the "Almighty is angry" at the Rotunda.[10] In spite of Jefferson's original desires, several faculty after the 1830s were men of the cloth. In 1835 a proposal was floated for "a church or a chapel in the Gothic style" to be placed on the Lawn immediately in front of the Rotunda.[11] Other chapel proposals followed, and in 1860 Pratt designed a Gothic chapel that would occupy the south end of the Lawn. The Civil War prevented the raising of funds for it.

The Civil War marked the nadir of the University's fortunes, but in the aftermath the University recovered and began a transformation. Used as a Confederate hospital, it narrowly escaped destruction when General George Armstrong Custer, on a Union cavalry raid through the area in March 1865, acceded to pleas to spare the town and the University. Custer, the first University "preservationist," was also swayed by his admiration for Jefferson as one of the nation's Founding Fathers. After the war, the University followed the national trend toward emphasizing science and technology in the curriculum. An experimental farm was laid out west of Monore Hill along McCormick Road in the early 1870s. To aid in the University's recovery and transformation, northern philanthropists in the

10   Reverend William Meade, *Sermon Delivered in the Rotunda of the University of Virginia on Sunday, May 24, 1829* (Charlottesville: F. Carr & Co., 1828), 21.
11   George Tucker to Joseph C. Cabell, Mary 18, 1835, Cabell Family Papers.

1870s gave funds for the McCormick Observatory and for the natural history museum at Brooks Hall.

The University finally got its chapel in the late 1880s, when the Ladies Chapel Aid Society and an Episcopal priest raised the money and commissioned University alumnus and Baltimore architect Charles E. Cassell to design it in a Gothic mode. Again, a Lawn location came under discussion, but the Board of Visitors chose to place it on the northwest side of the Rotunda. At the dedication ceremony, University Professor Maximilian Schele de Vere compared the "pagan temple" of the Rotunda to the "pointed window, the flying buttress, the pointed steeple . . . aspiring to heaven" of the chapel.[12]

The University Chapel balanced Brooks Hall Natural History Museum built on the other side of the Rotunda in 1876–1878. Brooks Hall bore little relation to the Jefferson compound; it was a thoroughly romantic and Victorian structure with high windows, mansard roof, names of famous scientists, and whimsical sculptures of animal heads, including a tapir. Its main comment on the Jefferson design was to indicate a new entrance to the Grounds, since its entrance faced West Main Street and toward the town of Charlottesville. A reorientation was taking place that would be completed in the University Beautiful.

University Beautiful (c. 1893–c. 1950)

Certainly, the 1880s hinted at the American Renaissance spirit that came to full flower with the World's Columbian Exposition in Chicago of 1893, but that world's fair, with its ensemble of classical buildings, murals, and statuary, brought it into full public view. This group of white beaux-arts buildings clustered around a lagoon in Chicago ushered in the so-called City Beautiful, or Urban Art, movement when cities such as Washington, DC (1901-02), Chicago (1906-09), and others were replanned along classical lines. Seen as a renewal of earlier European and American architectural, artistic, and urban planning traditions, the City Beautiful affected the American campus as well.

The University's inauguration to the University Beautiful coincides almost exactly with the Chicago fair. In 1892–94, Norfolk architect John Kevan Peebles, a University alumnus (1890), with his partner, James R. Carpenter, designed Fayerweather Gymnasium, utilizing what he claimed was a Jefferson-inspired style. Peebles made light reference to Jefferson's idiom: temple portico, red brick, and light-colored trim. But Peebles's accompanying rhetoric is impressive, for he condemns the University Chapel and Brooks Hall, and claims his building "follows the lines laid down by Jefferson."[13]

12   Maximilian Schele de Vere, *An Address delivered on the Occasion . . .* (Charlottesville: Jefferson Book and Job Publishing House, 1885), n.p.
13   John Kevan Peebles, "Thomas Jefferson, Architect," *American Architect and Building News* 47 (Jan. 19, 1895): 29–30; reprinted from "Thos. Jefferson, Architect,"*Alumni Bulletin* [University of Virginia], 1 (Nov. 1894): 68–74.

Rotunda, interior, 1896–1898, Stanford White

The fire of October 27, 1895, destroyed the Rotunda, ushering in designs by Stanford White. White, a principal of the New York architectural firm of McKim, Mead & White and a leading figure of the American Renaissance, rebuilt the Rotunda with a new interior, replaced the hated Mills Annex with a new north entrance portico, and filled in the south end of the Lawn with three buildings: Cabell, Cocke, and Rouss Halls. These new buildings reflected curriculum changes and the need for specialized engineering and science labs as well as the continuing desire for a public hall. White's work and the design decisions, such as the north entrance portico, and the filling in of the south end, were not his exclusively, but directed by the Board of Visitors and some faculty. White himself had reservations about the placement of the buildings at the south end and proposed a second scheme that kept the vista open. But Jefferson's intention that the visitor would proceed to the south and enter up the Lawn toward the Rotunda had never worked well; there was a steep slope, and it was out of the way. Also, immediately beyond the University's property to the south was a poor African-American housing area that was viewed as unsightly. White's buildings would block this from view.

White's work at the University helped bring to the fore Jefferson's plan as the paradigm for the new American university. Jefferson's architecture had been largely ignored since his death, but from the 1890s onward, esteem for his work rose. The plan of the University informed countless

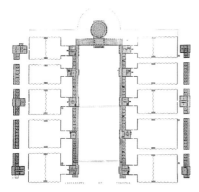

*University of Virginia, ground plan, 1822;
revised edition, 1825, John Neilson,
draughtsman; Peter Maverick, engraver*

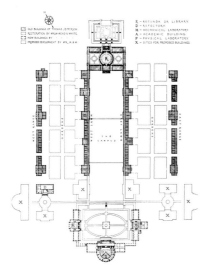

*Plan for the University, c. 1898–1910,
McKim, Mead and White*

plans for schools coast to coast but with one difference, and what White knew: the vast open space of the Lawn made people uncomfortable. In addition to the various schemes for chapels, other proposals included placing a statue of Jefferson and a Confederate victory arch at the end of the Lawn. White and the Board of Visitors saved the Lawn by enclosing it. Containment and the setting of limits became a nationwide trademark of the University Beautiful; at Virginia, walls and gates such as the Senff Gates by Henry Bacon were constructed.

Rebuilding the University in the late 1890s severely strained an institution with no real administration, no president, and that depended on the faculty chair and the rector of the Board of Visitors to oversee the operation. Chaos resulted, and McKim, Mead & White departed in a huff prior to completion in 1898, though they would return in 1905. As the American university was changing and professional schools and graduate programs were being instituted elsewhere, how would the University cope? In 1901 the first hospital—now a wing— was built after the designs of Paul Pelz, of Washington, DC. The Board of Visitors decided to create a strong, presidential administrative structure and to hire Edwin Anderson Alderman as the first president in 1904. In a sense an imperial presidency, Alderman's and the Board of Visitors' concept of the job can be seen in Carr's Hill, the President's House, with its giant columned portico designed by McKim, Mead & White.

Under Alderman's reign, 1904–1931, the University grew from 706 students in 1904 to 2,452 students in 1931, and specialized professional schools were instituted such as the Curry School of Education, the architecture department, and others. Planning for future expansion became important. White and his firm had projected a plan for the future expansion of the University that envisioned courts off to the side. This plan came to only partial fruition in buildings such as Randall Hall (1898–1899)

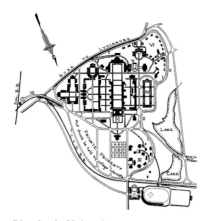

Plan for the University, 1913,
Warren Manning

by Paul Pelz, and Garrett Hall (1906–1908) by McKim, Mead & White. As a progressive, Alderman believed in professionals, and in 1906, Warren Manning, a landscape architect from Boston, began work on the Grounds. Manning produced two plans (1908, 1913), and with William Lambeth, the first published book on Jefferson as an architect.[14] Manning's penultimate scheme of 1913, which the University only partially followed, envisioned smaller courts and mini-lawns around the University.

Another dimension of the University Beautiful is the normalization of sports and athletics. Jefferson had intended the area underneath the terraces in front of the Rotunda as a gymnasium during inclement weather, but most activity would take place outdoors. By 1857, a gymnasium of two stories had been added onto the East Range, where students would exercise upon bars, ropes, dumbbells, and in sword play. Also the south end of the Lawn became an athletic field. Fayerweather Gym (1892–1894) was very different, a freestanding structure containing spaces for different types of activities. It became the first of many specialized indoor sports facilities at the University. Intercollegiate sports grew at the turn of the century and Lambeth Field (1911–1913), with its daunting colonnade by Robert E. Lee Taylor, amply showcases the renewed Roman classical fervor at the University.

The architectural idiom followed the precedent set by Peebles and White: red brick, white trim, and columns, in a style that would be variously called Colonial, Georgian, or Jefferson revival. Jefferson, of course, would not have thought of himself as a colonial, and to be a "Georgian" would have been an insult! Another feature of the campus beautiful was public art, hence murals and statues appear: a reproduction of Raphael's *School of Athens* by George Breck (1901) inside Cabell Hall, and *Homer* by Moses Ezekiel (1907) in front, statues of Jefferson by Ezekiel (1910) north of the Rotunda, and Karl Bitter (1915) on the Lawn, along with a reproduction of Houdon's *Washington* (1913); also on the Lawn, Gutzon Borglum's Aviator (1918) near Alderman Library, and Robert Aitken's *George Rogers Clark* (1921) on West Main Street, near the hospital.

Fiske Kimball, an architect, and already the author of *Thomas Jefferson, Architect* (1916), arrived in 1919 to head up the new architecture school (within the new McIntire School of Fine Arts) and he helped

---

14   William A. Lambeth and Warren H. Manning, *Thomas Jefferson as an Architect and a Designer of Landscape* (Boston: Houghton Mifflin, 1913).

inaugurate a system for architecture and planning based on collaboration that would control the university for the next twenty-five years. Kimball agreed with the already established direction of the University's architecture and planning. In addition to Jefferson, Kimball's heroes included McKim, Mead & White, who he believed had reinvigorated American architecture by returning it to a classic base. Perhaps because he lacked experience with large projects—having been within universities as a student or teacher—Kimball, followed a suggestion from Warren Manning, and asked well-established professional architects to join him in designing such buildings as Memorial Gymnasium. The already well known John Kevan Peebles joined Kimball, along with Walter Dabney Blair of New York and Robert E. Lee Taylor of Baltimore. Kimball left the University in 1923 to head up the Philadelphia Museum of Art, but he retained close ties to the University and the area for the remainder of his life, frequently critiquing designs. Following Kimball as head of architecture came Joseph Hudnut and A. Lawrence Kocher, who stayed only a few years, and then in 1927 Edmund S. Campbell, who remained until his death in 1950. The collaborative structure established for Memorial Gymnasium became institutionalized as the Board of Architects, or the Architectural Commission, and all the buildings for the next twenty years, a period of substantial growth, came through the hands of Campbell, Peebles, Taylor, and Blair.

Edmund Campbell, as the head of the architecture school, became the de facto "aesthetic conscience" of the University, and much of the consistency of the architecture can be attributed to him and the Board of Architects. The new reigning idiom, with minor exceptions, was a tamer Georgian Revival than the more bombastic and Roman-derived structures favored by White. The result was a substantial infrastructure of sound background buildings such as the Monroe Hill Dormitories, now Brown College (1928–29), which contain a series of small courtyards, and Monroe Hall. The University's focus on dormitories paralleled efforts of other universities to focus on student life in the 1920s. Additional buildings included Thornton Hall for the Engineering School (1930–35) and the initial stages of Scott Stadium (1929–31). More "foreground" buildings included Clark Hall (1930–32), with its mammoth portico for the Law School and its interior murals by Allyn Cox, and the giant Palladian motif entry of the Bayly Museum (1933–1935). Alderman Library (1936–38) was the last substantial building of this period. Even prior to the 1895 fire, Jefferson's circular library had come under criticism for the inability to be expanded. White's design vastly increased shelving space, but by 1917 it was filled and the University librarian asked for a new building. With the shift of the library out of the Rotunda to the new Alderman Library, a question arose—what to do with the old structure, the prime symbol of the University.

The University Beautiful and the various players from Stanford White to the Board of Architects had a unified vision of how a university should look. The result, although very different from Jefferson's in many ways, contained a cohesiveness, but one that was perhaps possible only with student enrollments of around 4,000.

Campus Suburban (c. 1950–c. 1976)

After World War II, America and university campuses became suburban. The causes at Virginia were several: growth, societal changes, and a new sense of excellence. The University of Virginia grew: for instance, the 1939 student population was 2,950; by 1949 it stood at 4,964; and ten years later, only 4,761; but by 1969, the population reached 9,735 students, and by 1979, it registered 16,464 students. Initially, the growth resulted from veterans returning from the war and taking advantage of the GI Bill; their children, the so-called baby boomers, followed them in the 1960s. And the University also changed its student admissions policy, thus its student profile. While women had been admitted in some of the graduate programs in the 1920s, the University had preserved the white male makeup of the undergraduate class and sent females off to Mary Washington College in Fredericksburg. Women became full citizens in 1970 and rapidly rose to one-half the student body. Virginia as a segregated society had routinely denied access to African Americans. They tentatively began to arrive in the 1950s, and more regularly in the later 1960s. In varying ways, most American institutions of higher learning during the post-World War II years, experienced similar growth and changes. The one major difference at the University lay with a sense of excellence.

Until the early 1960s the University remained a regional institution, though it claimed to be the "southern end of the Ivy League." It produced several Rhodes Scholars, and a few of the faculty had substantial reputations, but the University maintained its "preppy" image with students who wore coats and ties to class. Douglas Day, who later became a world-renowned literary scholar, recalled the University of the 1950s: "I joined one of the right fraternities (this was vital, clearly), bought the right kinds of clothes, played lacrosse (badly), got Gentlemen's C's, was never caught studying, and never let a professor know me well enough to connect my name with my face."[15] Although such behavior was a common feature of many universities in the 1950s, the University of Virginia's academic climate began to change in the 1960s. A new, more rigorous University began to flourish during the presidency Edgar Shannon from 1959 to 1974. Mandated to grow by the state legislature, in order to accommodate the baby boom population, Shannon, a former professor of English, hired eminent scholars, increased critical support facilities such as the library, and brought a new sense of scholarly rigor to the institution. The "gentleman's C" gave way as the University became one of the hot "public ivies." The

15   Douglas Day, *The Academical Village* (Charlottesville: Thomasson-Grant, 1982), 13.

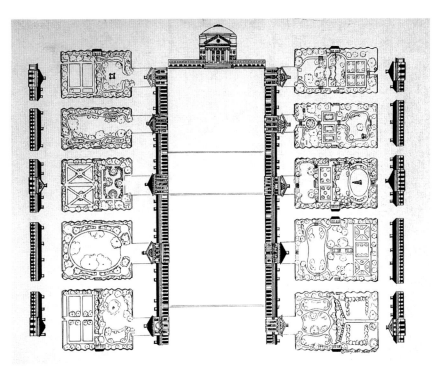

University of Virginia Academical Village, plan, c. 1960, Mary Hall Betts

state legislature, always relying on the University as the flagship of the state's educational system, provided significant funds for growth. Another factor perhaps was that the intense political activity that defined many American campuses in the late 1960s and early 1970s took only a mild form at Virginia.

The resultant building activity suburbanized the University. Changes occurred in the planning and design of buildings. Instead of the tight control of the Board of Architects, new bureaucratic layers tended to disperse the decision making, and in the end, nobody had an overall vision. Many of the decisions came through the department of Buildings and Grounds (later Facilities Management), and an endless series of committees set up for each new building. Initially, after World War II, Eggers and Higgins, the successor firm of John Russell Pope who designed the Jefferson Memorial and many classical beaux-arts buildings in Washington, DC, were the primary architects at the University. If anyone did, certainly Pope's old firm should have understood the University; but its design for Newcomb Hall—the student life center—while competent, lacked substance, and its addition to Cabell Hall—New Cabell Hall—was grossly insensitive. The University spread initially to the east, with many additions around the Hospital-Medical School, to west across Emmet Street, and along McCormick and Alderman Roads. The health sciences expanded as did the hard and applied sciences, which increasingly required immense laboratory-type spaces. The concept of the large—several-hundred-student—lecture course dates back to the late nineteenth century, but this notion increasingly shaped undergraduate courses. The flood of new buildings responded not only to specific curriculum needs but to a new concept of the university as a sort of suburban supermarket, in which courses under all sorts of labels are available to the consumer.

New architectural winds accompanied the suburban campus: Modernism in its many varieties set the new American style, and the University began to receive its share. One of the first signs was Gilmer Hall (1961–63) by Richmond architects Ballou and Justice, and Stainback and Scribner, whose main feature was a pierced concrete block screen, derived from Edward Durrell Stone and Minoru Yamasaki's work of the 1950s. A number of high-profile architects, Louis Kahn, Marcel Breuer, and Paul Rudolph, received commissions from the University, but for various reasons their designs remained unbuilt. Other eminent Modernists did succeed: Caudill Rowlett Scott (CRS) of Houston, known for its school work, designed Ruffner Hall (1970–73) on Emmet Street, a brick minimalist box for the Curry School of Education. A new focus on the arts led Shannon to break up the old art department, creating the School of Architecture, and then an art department that contained fine arts and art history. An acropolis of the arts was created behind Carr's Hill with new buildings for the Architecture School and the Drama department. Campbell Hall, or the Architecture School, and the linked Fiske Kimball Fine Arts Library (1965–70) by Sasaki, Dawson and DeMay of Boston, and Rawlings and Wilson of Richmond, with principal designer Kenneth DeMay and design consultant Pietro Belluschi, the architecture dean at MIT, abstracted modular elements of Jefferson's Lawn. A courtyard and large, suspended glass bays recall Jefferson as does the palette, a white concrete frame and red brick infill walls. Campbell Hall has a Bauhaus-styled "bridge" and lacks a clear main entry. In some cases attempts were made to create continuity between the various modern buildings such as with the architecture complex but overall, many buildings of this suburban period were conceived of as singular objects, each isolated in its environment.

The spatial environment can be described as increasingly suburban. Until the 1960s, the University's growth occurred adjacent to the Central Grounds; it may have been spread out, but still it was connected. A master plan produced by Sasaki, Dawson and DeMay in August 1965 envisioned expansion to the west, but no satellite campus. By 1968 plans were well under way for a satellite campus, "North Grounds," in which the spatial characteristic is really akin to an office park and the bus or the automobile became the major means of transportation. A bus system to transport students and staff between the increasingly far-flung campus began in 1971 with two buses; two more were added the next year.

The North Grounds satellite campus started innocently with a new sports complex, University or U Hall, and associated buildings (1960–65) by

Baskervill & Son of Richmond, with Anderson, Beckwith and Haible of Boston. The University had joined the Atlantic Coast Conference (ACC) and needed more space for spectators and parking. Acres of parking lots surrounded it, and major roads separated it from the rest of the University. Within four years, new buildings for the Law and Business School and student housing were envisioned far within the site, a good two-plus miles from the Academical Village. Designed and built between 1968 and 1975, after designs by Boston-based architect Hugh Stubbins, they were in a late International Style, almost indistinguishable from a corporate headquarters. Indicative of the suburban-modern attitude, the University slated Brooks Hall (1876–78), which had stood for a century, for demolition in the later 1970s, because it "did not look Jeffersonian" and failed to fit in. But an extensive protest led by architectural history students and supported by faculty brought a change of heart to the University administration and triggered—perhaps—a new era.

University Neotraditional (c. 1976–today).

An axiom of history, or at least contemporary culture, is that each generation tends to reject the immediate past of its parents and find new virtue in that of its grandparents. Certainly this appears true with the University in its turn to neotraditionalism in architecture, though as with any attempt to define the present day and recent trends, the perspective is limited. During exactly the same period (since c. 1976) another major shift involved the increasingly electronic university. The sudden and complete computer takeover has profound implications for the future of campus-based education. What relation the computer revolution has to neotraditionalism is unclear in fact, they may be polar opposites.

The University entered the final decades of the twentieth century riding on the crest of excellence begun by President Shannon, and then continued by Presidents Hereford, O'Neil, and Casteen. Plans were put forward in the late 1970s and early 1980s to pursue the satellite model by removing the hospital and medical school to sites outside of town, and creating remote housing campuses for the students. For various reasons, including a reduction in funding by the state and internal opposition, this did not happen. And shifts in architectural ideology, such as postmodernism, the emergence of the historic preservation ethic on a national scale, and a new appreciation of the past, contributed to the shift in architectural emphasis at the University, along with new administrative structures.

How much the national neotraditional trend is tied to the conservative political trends of the 1980s and 1990s is difficult to assess. Certainly debates have raged on university campuses and at Virginia over the nature of higher education, and the new perspectives of gender and multiculturalism, versus a fact-based curriculum in the liberal arts. After all, E. D. Hirsch, author of *Cultural Literacy* (1987), which is a call for a return to fact-based education, is on the faculty of Virginia.

During the Architecture School deanship of Jaquelin Robertson (1981–88), the original Academical Village received new attention in fundraising and in a new approach to its care. J. Murray Howard, an architect and historian, became the curator of the Lawn and embarked on a campaign to restore accurately rather than simply maintain. Robertson also brought as designers a group of postmodern architects, who were sympathetic to the historical fabric, such as Robert A. M. Stern's additions to Observatory Hill Dining Hall (1984), R. M. Kliment and Frances Halsband's Gilmer Hall Addition (1984–87), Hartman-Cox's additions to Monroe Hall (1984–87), and Michael Graves's Bryan Hall (1990–95).

Shifts in vision came slowly. Intimations of the neotraditional campus existed prior to 1976, and elements of the suburban ethos continued well past that date. During the suburban period, University architectural historians William B. "Pete" O'Neal and Frederick Doveton Nichols focused new scholarly attention on Jefferson's work. The gardens of the pavilions were imaginatively re-created in a Colonial manner by Alden Hopkins in the 1950s and 1960s. Nichols led a campaign to restore the interior of the Rotunda, and between 1973 and 1975 an approximation of Jefferson's was created. The question does remain of what purpose it might serve? and what to do with it? Alternatively, and visible from all over town, is the new high-rise University Hospital (1987–89), by Metcalf with Davis Brody and Russo and Sonder. Resembling minimalist sculpture with its simple form and sleek skin of white enamel panels and glazing, it appears as an alien, New York intruder, having nothing to do with Jefferson's architecture. Hereford College (1990–92), by Tod Williams and Billie Tsein from New York and VMDO of Charlottesville, is also modern; yet it is a thoughtful rethinking of the serialism implicit in the original siting of the Academical Village. The individual dormitory units march up the hillside while remaining focused on the dining hall with its canopy entrance. The entrance cutouts and the brickwork and wrap-around corner windows recall Dutch housing of the 1920s and 1930s.

The New York architectural press admired Hereford College, while many at the University, including members of the Board of Visitors, criticized it.[16] The neotraditionalist solution of mimicking the past was not always effective, as demonstrated by the attempt to clothe a parking garage with Colonial details. The overblown Central Grounds Parking Garage and University Bookstore (1989–94), by Walker Parking Consultants with Mariani & Associates, in which the parking engineers acted as the primary designers, illustrated that Colonial forms could (and should) be stretched only so far.

Robert A. M. Stern's University designs, especially the Colgate Darden Business School (1992–96), represent the most obvious return to

---

16   Paul Goldberger, "Jefferson's Legacy: Dialogues With the Past," *New York Times*, May 23, 1993: 33.

tradition. A full-bore neo-Jeffersonian revival and a direct refutation of the Business School's former home, the overall impact is of a too-loud pretentiousness. Although in many ways the forms and details recall Jefferson, and the south courtyard with pavilions reminiscent of Pavilion IX at the Lawn is particularly well done, the school resembles a neotraditional office park: over-scaled, anonymous, and dropped arbitrarily on its site from outer space. The Darden swaggers, lacking the grace of Jefferson's Lawn.

These problems, along with dispersed decision-making authority and the lack of an agreed-upon vision, led Harry W. Porter Jr., dean of the School of Architecture (1988–93), to propose in 1991 the establishment of the architect for the University. Porter initially took the position and was followed in 1995 by Samuel A. "Pete" Anderson III. Porter and the University did not intend the architect to be a design office but to assist the president and the Board of Visitors in ensuring the continuation of Jefferson's vision for the University grounds and to act as the aesthetic conscience. The University architect is concerned with selecting architects and landscape architects, as well as what buildings should be built, and where. At present, the architect's office, with Ayers Saint Gross of Baltimore, and Michael Vergason Landscape Architects, is creating a new masterplan that attempts to unify the sprawling suburban growth with infill development and a network of pedestrian-oriented circulation.

In some ways the history of the University of Virginia's campus, or Grounds as it is fondly known, mirrors that of other similar institutions. All can identify their own picturesque, campus beautiful, and suburban periods, and many are experiencing their own versions of neotraditionalism, or a search for roots. And each is unique. At the University of Virginia, perhaps more than any other American university, a palpable sense of time can really grasp the spectator. It is powerful, and the dialogue with history and especially with Thomas Jefferson, the original designer, and his intentions can degenerate into mimicry and obtuseness, or inspire creativity. How to retain some part of the original vision in what has become cyber-reality and an electronic village remains a pressing concern.

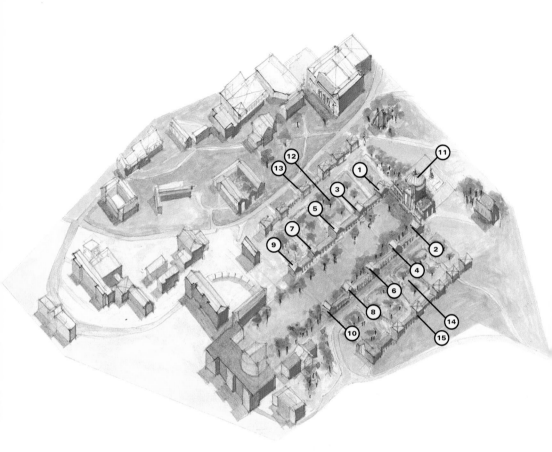

Thomas Jefferson's
Academical Village

Thomas Jefferson's design for the University of Virginia can be traced to numerous sources, but perhaps the ultimate inspiration came from his studies at the College of William and Mary in Williamsburg between 1760 and 1762. During the years of his attendance, all the college's students and faculty lived, ate, slept, studied, and attended classes in one large structure, today called the Wren Building. Life in the building was chaos, characterized by food fights and drunkenness—by students and faculty. Six of the seven faculty were Anglican clergy. Several were unmarried and supposedly celibate, yet fathered illegitimate children. One of the clergy faculty liked to lead his young charges on drunken raids against the townspeople of Williamsburg. This type of behavior and the single large building were not uncommon at many American colleges. Hence when Jefferson later described his ideal college, it was based on personal background. He wrote in 1810: "It is infinitely better to erect a small and separate lodge for each separate professorship, with only a hall below for his class, and two chambers above for himself, joining these lodges by barracks for a certain portion of the students, opening into a covered way to give a dry communication between all the schools. The whole of these, arranged around an open square for grass and trees, would make it, what it should be in fact, an academical village."

Jefferson's initial scheme for the Albemarle Academy in 1814 was a U-shaped quadrangle of about 750 feet across, open at one end, and surrounded by nine pavilions for teaching and professor's lodging. The students were to be housed in single-room dormitories between the pavilions. It was a paper scheme ideal for a large, flat plain. In mid-1817 the site for the future university was acquired, a narrow ridge bordered by two roads, with a stream at one side. His 1814 plan would not fit and he modified it, creating rows of eight pavilions and dormitories facing each other 200 feet apart. He fit parallel rows onto the site by grading to make three terraces. On July 18, 1817, Jefferson surveyed the site, laid out the parallel rows of buildings, and noted that "some principal building" would be placed in the center of the north terrace.

Jefferson's concept of the "principal building" resulted from his inquiries in mid–1817 to William Thornton and Benjamin Henry Latrobe, two of his architectural colleagues (and bitter enemies unto one another). His letters contained a sketch of the earlier Lawn scheme, but his primary motive was to gain advice on the facades of the pavilions, for they should be "models of taste and good architecture, and of a variety of appearance, no two alike, so as to serve as specimens for the Architectural lecturer." Jefferson had recently sold his extensive library, including the books on architecture, to the Library of Congress, and was without references. In the years to come, Jefferson repurchased several architecture books, including Giacomo Leoni's edition of Palladio. Thornton replied with two drawings for the facades suggesting that the central pavilion should receive more emphasis, and replacing the square piers in front of the dormitories with columns. Jefferson combined Thornton's facade and his own 1814 prototypical facade for the first pavilion built (VII), whose cornerstone was laid in October 1817.

Latrobe suggested a number of different facades for the pavilions, several of which contained giant-order porticos, and at the center, a large domed structure serving as a focal point. Jefferson adopted these ideas in the next several pavilions to be erected, and Latrobe's domed building became a library and classrooms, or the Rotunda. Jefferson had previously, around 1791, suggested a cylindrical domed structure for the US Capitol in Washington, DC. Its plan was close to that of the Rotunda. The exact circumstances surrounding this design are unclear, but two of his drawings have survived.

Jefferson refined the design in the years following, some of which were motivated by political reasons. In late 1818, as the result of a state legislature meeting on higher education, the number of professorships at the university rose to ten, and Jefferson added two pavilions, making ten altogether. However, he had already graded the site and created the terraces, and construction had begun. His 1817 plan for the University had four pavilions on each side, with dormitory rooms flanking the end pavilions. In 1818 he had to rearrange the pavilions. Instead of dormitories flanking and terminating each side, pavilions became the major terminating feature at the north end (Pavilions I and II), while at the south end, instead of eight dormitories beyond the last pavilions, now there was only one. The consequence was that pavilions at the north end (nos. I, II, III, and IV) were pushed into the line, and the spacing became irregular between them. The distance across the Lawn was constant at the top as at the bottom—200 feet—but the intervals between the pavilions widened toward the south—or open—end. The result, combined with the 42-inch drop of each terrace, created a foreshortened appearance, so the distance to the Rotunda appeared greater from the south. From the Rotunda, the opposite effect occurred, and the last pavilion appeared closer. The famous "perceptual shift" is really a result of site and politics.

Jefferson controlled the design but did take a few suggestions, such as one by board member Joseph Cabell proposed moving the gardens between the pavilions and the outer row of dormitories and hotels. At first Jefferson resisted, but on reflection recognized the merits and simply cut out the old portion of his original drawing and taped in the new design. He preferred scarce lined graph paper, and his wrist—which he had broken earlier in life—pained him. He reported on the change in the ground plan: "I think it a real improvement, and the greater, as by throwing the Hotels and additional dormitories on a back street, it forms in fact the commencement of a regular town, capable of being enlarged to any event which future circumstances may call for." By July 1819, Jefferson had modified the plan even more by drawing in the serpentine walls.

At some point during later 1817, Jefferson acquired several architectural books, including several works by Palladio and James Gibbs, and Charles-Edouard Errard and Roland Fréart de Chambray's *Parallèle de l'Architecture Antique avec la Moderne* (1766). One of the Palladio books, Giacomo Leoni's edition of *The Architecture of A. Palladio* (1742), was a favorite for years, Jefferson had used extensively at Monticello. His preference was well known; for instance, a friend reported to one of the members of the Board of Visitors: "With Mr. Jefferson I conversed at length on the subject of architecture—Palladio he said 'was the Bible'—you should get it and stick close to it. . . . " These two books provided most of the external details for the different pavilion facades and the Rotunda. For the colonnade on the Lawn, Jefferson used the Tuscan order, the most solid and rustic order of antiquity. Although Jefferson viewed the Tuscan order as "too plain" and "not fit for a dwelling House," he chose it because of its lack of ornament and supposed simplicity of construction. Jefferson probably turned to Jombert's *Architecture de Palladio* (1764), a small volume that he owned and praised as being "portable," and more easily used in the field in contrast to large folios. In a drawing Jefferson attempted to make the Tuscan order more elegant by elongating it to a height of more than nine times the lower diameter, instead of the more orthodox proportion of seven to one. The milk-bottle shape of some of the Tuscan columns—or their exaggerated entices, which is the convex curve or bulge of the shaft—resulted from both the workmen misjudging the proportions and later subsequent coats of plaster and paint.

All of the columns on the Lawn were constructed of specially molded brick and then covered with skim coats of a plaster type of stucco. Probably, they were left the natural color of the stucco, a light tan, or buff. The white paint that covers them came later in the nineteenth century. Several Tuscan columns of the colonnade—near Pavilion VIII—were restored in 1998. The capitals and bases of the colonnade appear to be of a local quartzite stone; John Gorman, who had worked for Jefferson at Monticello, carved most of them. Gorman also provided some of the bases and capitals of the more complicated pavilions.

Modifications altered the design of the pavilions. Initially, Jefferson saw the professors as celibate, or not having families since his 1814 floor plan and the plan for the first pavilion (VII) had the professor living in two rooms on the second floor over the classroom. The basement contained cooking and storage spaces. The pavilion would measure 36 feet across and 24 feet deep. Objections must have arisen because Jefferson's designs for later pavilions show larger and more spacious quarters for the professor. In many cases the ground floor is split into several rooms. The different facades follow no discernible scheme; the motifs are not linked to the disciplines housed within. Instead, the motifs of five of the facades are drawn from Palladio and hence are modern, and five are drawn from Chambray and represent antiquity. Jefferson described his respect for antiquity when he wrote in 1824:

"antiquity has left us the finest models for imitation; and he who studies and imitates them most nearly, will nearest approach the perfection of the art." But the University was also modern, and the consequence is that down the Lawn copies of the ancient orders from Errard and Fréart de Chambray are opposed by modern copies from Palladio, but they are not all lined up on one side; instead they are intermixed.

Jefferson's drawings of the pavilions ignore the second-floor balconies and their Chinese Chippendale railings. Why this is so remains unclear; he clearly intended for the faculty who lived on the second floor to have communication with each other across the intervening dormitory roofs. The faculty, in other words, had a means of communication separate from the students. John Neilson, who produced a brilliant series of watercolor renderings of the Lawn, did include them. Another Jefferson feature has disappeared, the original "rooflets," or a ridge and gutter scheme for the roofs on the dormitories. In spite of objections from many sources that such flat roofs would leak, Jefferson insisted on them. They did leak and now pitched roofs with slate shingles covers the dormitories.

Initially, Jefferson, who was 74 years old in 1817, acted as the supervisor of construction. He not only laid out the village and designed the buildings but he wrote exacting specifications and calculated the materials such as the number of bricks for each pavilion. In addition to establishing a brickyard and purchasing lumber, hardware, glass, and other items, he hired the builders. In April 1817, he wrote to James Dinsmore, an Irish-born joiner who had worked on Monticello, to join the construction team and to bring along John Neilson. Neilson, also Irish born and a superior joiner, had talents as a renderer and produced the so-called Maverick ground plan of 1822 along with a wonderful set of watercolor elevations of the buildings. Captain James Oldham served as a carpenter at Monticello between 1801 and 1808, and worked on Pavilion I. Jefferson's commitment to the University drew wonder, for as his Monticello overseer recalled years later: "he rode there from Monticello every day while the University was building, unless the weather was very stormy. I don't think he ever missed a day unless the weather was very bad." But ultimately the supervision proved too much and on March 3, 1819, Arthur S. Brockenbrough arrived to take over as proctor and direct the building campaign.

The construction workmen supplied their own working "draughts," or drawings for many of the details. The result is that many interior details are not designed by Jefferson but by workmen. In 1819 a group of Philadelphia builders led by Richard Ware arrived and began building the pavilions on the east side. Other talented craftsmen were imported for this large construction job, such as English immigrant William John Coffee of New York. Joseph Antrim, an Irishman who directed the plastered interiors and plasterwork of the pavilions and Rotunda. Jefferson hoped that native American stone could be employed for the capitals of several of the pavilions and hence he engaged the stone cutters, Michele and Giacomo Raggi from

Italy. Problems arose, the Raggis drank too much wine and the native Aquia stone was too porous and soft. They returned to Italy and helped supply capitals and bases out of Carrara marble.

At least 200 individuals worked in the University's construction, some known, others anonymous. African-American freedmen and slaves worked on the project, primarily in grading and leveling. Several women were employed as housekeepers for the construction crews. Dinsmore and Neilson were master carpenters involved in the more delicate details of the construction. Brickmasons performed a special trade; at its peak, the brickyard west of the Lawn produced 180,000 bricks a month. Even so, the demands were greater and the University purchased 300,000 bricks from John M. Perry. Most of the brickwork on the Lawn is laid up in a Flemish bond, alternating stretchers and headers for the walls; below the water table English bond is more prominent. Here and there, other variations such as common bond appear.

Construction lasted over nine long years, with activity bustling from spring to late fall. The west pavilions and dormitories came first, followed in 1819 by the east side of the Lawn. In 1820 the outer line of hotels and dormitories took shape. The Rotunda came last; it was the most expensive building, and the state legislature agitated for Jefferson to open the University prior to its funding. He held off, knowing that in the eyes of a penurious legislature, an operating university would not need such an imposing structure. Final funding came through in February 1823, and the Rotunda's construction began; it was finished in 1826.

Jefferson's concept for landscaping the Lawn indicated "grass & trees" but he never specified the exact form in drawings or correspondence. In 1823, University proctor Arthur Brockenbrough purchased 100 young locusts and 116 young poplars. Their disposition is uncertain, for several of the early prints show no trees. However, the images in these prints date prior to 1823. By 1830, Professor John A. G. Davis noted "the double row of young locust trees, which had been planted on each side of the Lawn, which were giving promise of shade in years to come." Over the years these were replaced, and today most of the Lawn is planted with a double row of ash trees.

Jefferson's drawings and those of John Neilson and other early observers depict an idealized Lawn. In actuality, modifications began early and have continued. Outhouses, storage sheds, and other structures were erected back in the gardens and behind the neat lines of pavilions and colonnades. Classrooms on the ground floor disrupted the faculty inhabitants, and gradually the classrooms became living quarters or administrative offices, sometimes taking over the entire pavilion. And the pavilions received additions at the rear. Beginning in the 1970s all of the pavilions with the exception of VII—the Colonnade Club—were returned to faculty living quarters and teaching functions resumed in Pavilion VIII. An extensive restoration of the pavilions is under way during 1998–99.

Students have always lived in the dormitory rooms, both on the

Lawn and in the ranges. The number of students per room has varied over the years; Jefferson intended two students per room, and for much of the time this ratio was followed. Students who paid a supplement could have a single room. In the mid-1960s, all the Lawn and Range rooms were converted to single occupancy. Jefferson provided fireplaces for each room and the piles of wood next to each door testify to their continuing use. Hygienic facilities were located around to the rear and in outhouses. Today, all of the dormitory rooms have wash basins, steam heating, and electricity. However, as confirmed by the frequent sight of students in bathrobes walking back and forth, bathing facilities and restrooms, remain in the rear in the basement. Living on the Lawn is viewed as a high privilege, and competition for rooms is fierce.

Letters near the end of his life tell of the pride Jefferson felt in the University. To his aging lady friend in France, Maria Cosway, he boasted: "It would be thought a handsome and classical thing in Italy." To William Short he wrote: "It will be a splendid establishment, would be thought so in Europe, and for the chastity of its architecture and classical taste leaves everything in America far behind it." To a political associate he wrote: "Withdrawn by age from all other public services and attentions to public things, I am closing the last scenes of life by fashioning and fostering an establishment for the instruction of those who are to come after us. I hope its influence on their virtue, freedom, fame and happiness, will be salutary and permanent. The form and distributions of its structure are original and unique, the architecture chaste and classical, and the whole well worthy of attracting the curiosity of a visit."

In one sense, the University embodied Jefferson's ideals and his accomplishments. He dictated that his tombstone at Monticello be inscribed: "Here was buried Thomas Jefferson Author of the Declaration of American Independence of the Statute of Virginia for Religious Freedom and Father of the University of Virginia." He omitted political offices, but instead sought recognition for his two writings, which are fundamental to American freedom, and the institution by which they would be carried out.

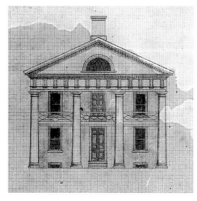

Study for Pavilion I, 1819,
Thomas Jefferson

Pavilion I

Roland Frèart de Chambray and Charles Errard, Parallèle de l'Architecture Antique avec le Moderne *(1766), Plate III*

Pavilion I, detail of capital and entablature

1. Pavilion I   *Thomas Jefferson, 1819–1822*

Begun as part of the 1819 building campaign and finished in 1822, Pavilion I was actually the third pavilion to be constructed (and the seventh to be completed). The construction team included carpenter James Oldham, Curtis Carter, and brickmason William Phillips (whose brickwork Jefferson claimed "the best work done there"). Jefferson's drawing for this pavilion exhibits his resourcefulness, for after he had laid out the facade and floor plans on his graph paper he realized he had no room for the chimney. Hence, he drew separately the missing chimney and glued it to the top of the paper. Jefferson identified the facade's orders as Doric of Diocletian's Baths in Rome, as according to Chambray and Errard's book. Roman rather than Greek Doric meant that the columns had bases, here cut from native stone by John Gorman, who made the capitals as well. Jefferson spaced the four columns spaced widely apart, creating, in contrast to the next pavilion, a sense of openness. This wide-spaced columnar arrangement defines a Jefferson trademark. The frieze caused some trouble for he had to explain it to William Coffee, who modeled and cast it: "You are right in what you have thought and done as to the metopes of our Doric pavilion. Those of the baths of Diocletian are all human faces and so are to be those of our Doric pavilion." Faces of Apollo, the Roman god of agriculture, appear between the triglyphs.

Cast-iron tie rods from the ceiling supported the balcony with the Chippendale railing, a structural system Jefferson saw on his travels. One of these tie rods gave way during commencement exercises in May 1997, causing a fatal accident. The rods here and on the other pavilions have since been replaced. The pavilion's three-bayed facade leads to a central hall and two rooms on the ground floor. Typical of Jefferson's disdain of staircases as a major architectural feature, the staircase is pushed into the front left-hand corner and cuts across a window.

The first occupant of Pavilion I was Dr. John Patton Emmet, who came to the United States at the age of eight from Dublin, Ireland. One of the original eight professors, he had studied abroad and was teaching in South Carolina when Jefferson hired him to teach natural history and chemistry. Jefferson added to his teaching subjects zoology, geology, and mineralogy. Emmet kept animals and snakes in the pavilion and asked Jefferson to add a room for lectures and experiments. Known for his charm, Emmet married Mary Byrd Tucker, a niece of George Tucker, who taught moral philosophy. Emmet became taken by plant experimentation and purchased land west of the University where he built a house named Morea and moved there in 1834.

2. Pavilion II *Thomas Jefferson, 1819–1822*

Jefferson designed this pavilion and the others on the east side of the Lawn after June 5th, 1819. On that day he wrote to Arthur Brockenbrough, the proctor: "As it is but lately concluded to commence the Eastern range of pavilions & Dormitories I have not prepared the plans, nor shall I be at leisure to turn to that business till the week after the ensuing one, but those pavilions will vary so little from the dimensions last given, & those of No I, II, III of the Western range that if the foundations are dug to that, the trimming of them to what shall be the exact size of each will be trifling." Within three weeks he had produced the basic design for each.

Jefferson identified the source for this pavilion as the Ionic of

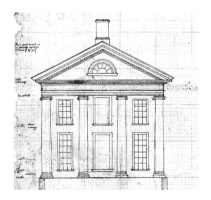 

Study for Pavilion II, June 1819,　　　　　*Pavilion II*
Thomas Jefferson

Pavilion II, detail of capital and entablature

Fortuna Virilis, Rome, from Palladio. Facing Pavilion II across the Lawn stood the Doric order of Pavilion I; the Rotunda would be Corinthian; hence, within a few steps at the end of the Lawn clustered the three great orders of antiquity. The columns are pushed forward slightly from the smaller colonnade, giving the facade great emphasis. Its Ionic capitals were carved in Italy from Carrara marble and have three eggs between the volutes. The outer corner volutes angled out. John Gorman provided the Ionic column bases. The entablature is drawn from Fortuna Virilis, showing in the lower or architrave level a plain fascia and egg and dart moldings, then for the frieze, cherubs, ox skulls, and a linking garland motif, and then the cornice of dentils.

The pavilion's construction commenced in 1819 under the direction of Richard Ware from Philadelphia. An indication of the materials involved can be gleaned from the records kept by Proctor Brockenbrough. Ware supplied 115,267 common bricks, 3,731 bricks for the columns and foundations, and 8,269 oil stock bricks—a special facing brick—for the front facade. In addition, William Phillips brought in bricks for the back wall. The pavilion was completed by 1822, and Dr. John Patton Emmet lived in it in 1825, but then moved to Pavilion I. The first permanent resident was Thomas Johnson, who taught anatomy and surgery.

3. Pavilion III *Thomas Jefferson, 1818–1821*

Pavilion III was the second of the pavilions to be begun, construction beginning in 1818 and finished by 1821. The construction team consisted of master carpenter John Dinsmore, who had worked on Monticello, brickmason John Perry, and bricklayer Matthew Brown. The facade design sprang from Benjamin Henry Latrobe's suggestion for giant two-story orders, which Jefferson labeled "Corinthian Palladio." Jefferson squeezed the columns together, creating a tighter composition than seen in the other two-story orders. In addition to satisfying Jefferson's desire for variety, the squeezed portico permitted space for two more pavilions on the Lawn, one to each side. Behind the portico stood a five-bayed facade with the typical large windows Jefferson preferred.

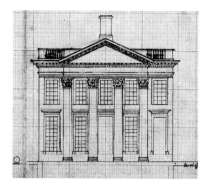

Study for Pavilion III, c.1818,
Thomas Jefferson

Pavilion III

  The Corinthian capitals carved of Carrara marble in Italy came up the James River by bateau and then continued by oxcart to the University. Above them, the soffit holds carved wooden modillions with acanthus leaves, which are repeated in the pediment. Egg and dart moldings and dentils complete the ensemble. On the interior many of the details bear a strong similarity to those Dinsmore had executed at Monticello.

  This pavilion's floor plan diverged from Jefferson's original: the classroom was entered at the center bay, while the professor's apartments opened into a door in the far right bay. In addition to the second floor's three rooms, the professor had a small room at the rear on the first floor. Jefferson intended that Francis Walker Gilmer, who was recruiting faculty in Europe, would be the first resident as head of the law school. But Gilmer died prior to taking up the position and the first resident was John Taylor Lomax, the only native Virginian amongst the initial faculty. Later in the nineteenth century an addition was made to the rear. The pavilion served for a period as administrative offices in addition to housing faculty. The University recently restored it.

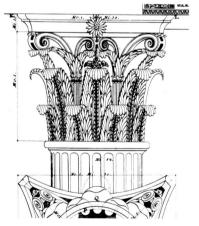

Giacomo Leoni, Architecture of
A. Palladio: In Four Books *(1742),*
Plate XXVI

Pavilion III, detail of capital and
entablature

Jefferson's notes on his drawing for Pavilion IV indicate the source for the facade as "Doric of Albano," which he drew from Chambray and Errard. The entablature has large triglyphs with guttae, and then in the soffit of the fascia wonderful guttae blocks, each with twenty-eight pegs. Jefferson's attempt to provide "specimens for the Architectural lecturer," went so far as to change the pattern in the mutton of the pediment lunette window from the neighboring Pavilion II and to use two different schemes for the Chinese Chippendale railing on the balcony.

Study for Pavilion IV, June 1819, Thomas Jefferson

The original plan called for a central entrance into the ground-floor classroom and two triple-sash windows on each side. Sometime after the classroom function was given up, the entrance was moved to the extreme right-hand window and the central door became a window. Ware of Philadelphia headed the construction team.

The first residents were Mr. and Mrs. George Blaettermann, he from Germany, she from England. He,

Pavilion IV

at age 43, was the oldest of the first professors. He specialized in modern languages, and could teach nine. But he couldn't get along with anybody— neither the faculty nor his wife, whom he apparently beat with regularity. One of his outrageous acts was to paint the front of the pavilion and still today, traces of the red paint remain. He was dismissed from the faculty in 1840. Maximilian Schele de Vere, a professor of modern languages and a great cosmopolitan figure, lived here for 51 years. Between 1904 and 1950 this pavilion served as the office of the president.

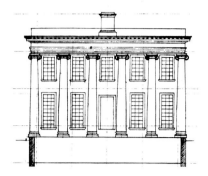

Study for Pavilion V, c.1818,
Thomas Jefferson.

Pavilion V

5. Pavilion V   *Thomas Jefferson, 1818–1821*

Benjamin Latrobe suggested the facade for Pavilion V. Jefferson wrote on his drawing: "Palladio's Ionic order, with modillions." Pavilion VI was the fourth pavilion to be built. Work began in 1818, and the construction team, headed by master carpenter John Dinsmore and brickmason John Perry, completed it by 1821. Here, Jefferson indulges in an orgy of columns, the six widely spaced giant-order Ionic columns imbue it with great presence on the Lawn. The Ionic capitals were part of the Italian commission and of Carrara marble. The volutes of the capitals have a thin band of egg and dart molding above. The entablature is relatively plain, long linear bands of raised molding and a row of egg and dart, but the cornice has modillion blocks laced with rosettes. The bases were by the local stonecutter John Gorman.

The plan is standard for Jefferson: a central hall, two rooms on the main floors, and a staircase unceremoniously pushed into a corner. The initial occupant was 24-year-old George Long from Trinity College, Cambridge, who was hired to teach ancient languages. He arrived in December 1824, and soon met with Jefferson, whom he described as a "tall dignified old gentleman." Long wrote years later: "I was pleased with his simple Virginia dress, and his conversation free from affectation."

6. Pavilion VI   *Thomas Jefferson, 1819–1822*

Begun in 1819 and finished in 1822, except for plastering, Pavilion VI was constructed under the direction of Richard Ware from Philadelphia, and brickmason Curtis Carter. In a sense, this is the simplest of the pavilions. Jefferson omitted a large order and did not recess the center of the facade as with Pavilions VIII and IX. Instead, it gains its distinction through refinement. Jefferson identified the source for the facade's details as Ionic, Theater of Marcellus, Rome, as shown in Errard and Chambray. The pavilion's

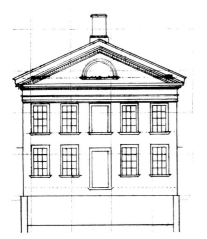

Study for Pavilion VI, June 1819,
Thomas Jefferson

Pavilion VI

Interior, Pavilion VI

entablature features a series of moldings, and prominent dentils are underlined by an egg and dart molding. A radiating pattern decorates the lunette window in the pediment. The Tuscan colonnade steps forward a few feet at ground level to create an appropriate porch. In contrast to many of the other pavilions, the windows on this one are smaller, with a double-hung sash. Louvered blinds were included.

Charles Bonnycastle, a 28-year-old Englishman trained at the Royal Military Academy, arrived in February 1825 to take up residence as the chair of natural philosophy. After two years he transferred to mathematics. He married Ann Mason Tutt of Loudoun County, known for her beauty. Well-liked he was chair of the faculty from 1833 to 1835 and died in 1840.

7. Pavilion VII *Thomas Jefferson, 1817–1819*

The first pavilion to be built, Pavilion VII, was the site of the cornerstone-laying ceremony on October 6, 1817. The Richmond Enquirer reported the attendance of Jefferson, Monroe and Madison, and that the local Freemasons performed; the laying of the stone had "all the ceremony and solemnity due to such an occasion." Jefferson's drawing for the pavilion identified it as "Doric Palladio." The actual design combines Jefferson's initial 1814 scheme for a pavilion and William Thornton's suggestions of mid-1817. The only stacked facade on the Lawn, a five-bayed arcade holds up a second floor of six Roman Doric columns and a pediment with a lunette window. In contrast to the other facades it is more visually complicated, an effect that evidently did not please Jefferson, for he never repeated it. However, the composition looked back both to his earlier schemes for Monticello, and also Poplar Forest.

Brickmason John Perry and Chisholm headed the building of Pavilion VII, and carpenter John Dinsmore and joiner John Neilson

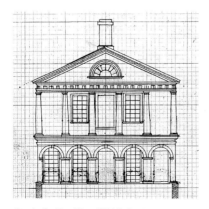

Study for Pavilion VII, July 1817,
Thomas Jefferson

Pavilion VII

Detail, Colonnade Club door,
Pavilion VII

provided many of the wood details. The original plan had on the first floor a central entrance into the classroom, and then a side entrance to the stairwell for the faculty apartment. Today, only the side entrance survives. The pavilion served as the temporary library for the University, and an upstairs room with an elaborate frieze served that purpose. Typically, the upstairs rooms, which served as living quarters, received more decoration than the lower-floor classrooms. As a consequence of being the first pavilion and initially the library, Pavilion VII became the unofficial faculty center, with informal meetings and the site where reprimands would be issued against the rebellious students. Beginning in 1832, the students and faculty established a University chaplain, and religious services were held on the ground floor. An extension in 1856 added several rooms and reoriented the staircase. In 1907 it became the Colonnade Club, a social center for faculty, alumni, and friends of the University. Another extension added more rooms for overnight guests. The current restoration will be completed during the year 2000.

8. Pavilion VIII   *Thomas Jefferson, 1819–1822*

Jefferson identified the source for the orders on this pavilion as from Chambray and Errard and their rendition of Corinthian of Diocletian's Baths, Rome. However, in his specification book he wrote, "Latrobe's Lodge front," indicating that either Latrobe supplied the design—which has been lost—or Jefferson copied it. The only Latrobe design on the east Lawn, it sits across from Thornton's contribution and the modern Palladio. Square and blocky, the entrance is recessed and contains two Corinthian columns in antis, and two engaged columns at the corner, all two stories in height. The wonderful capitals with their highly detailed acanthus leaves were cut in Italy. The elaborate cornice executed by William Coffee, has modillions, egg and dart molding, and dentils. At ground level, the Tuscan colonnade steps forward several feet, and at the same time creates a slightly different rhythm so as to distinguish the facade and to create a porch. Because of the recess, the second floor access to the roof of the colonnade is across a small bridge. This is the only pavilion with arched windows; they occur at the ground

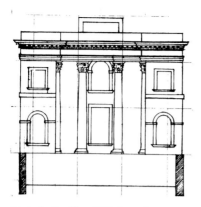

Study for Pavilion VIII, June 1819,
Thomas Jefferson

Pavilion VIII

level and are masked by the colonnade. Jefferson's drawing shows a parapet that hid the roof, however that was removed because of drainage and a
hipped roof substituted. The roof of Pavilion VIII has been restored to show
Jefferson's original tin shingles. The construction team consisted of master
carpenter Joiner John Dinsmore, brickmason John Perry, and Abiah B.
Thorn, who was part of the Philadelphia building crew.

Professor and Mrs. Thomas Hewett Key were the initial residents of
Pavilion VIII. Arriving in February 1825, Key's degrees were from Cambridge
and he had studied medicine in London. However, his chair was mathematics. He remained only two years before returning to England to become a
professor of Latin at the University of London. A later resident, whose
exploits are commemorated in a plaque on the pavilion William H. Echols
tried to save the Rotunda during the fire of 1895 by dynamiting the connec-

tion with the Annex. Beginning in the
1950s this pavilion served as the office
of the president of the University. In
1984 the president's office was moved
to Madison Hall and the pavilion was
restored as a teaching pavilion with
classrooms on the ground floor and
basement, and two faculty apartments
upstairs.

Pavilion VIII, detail of capital and
entablature

Pavilion IX

9. Pavilion IX   *Thomas Jefferson, 1818–1822*

Frequently photographed and speculated on by students of Jefferson's architecture, Pavilion IX is probably the most famous pavilion on the Lawn. The reasons involve its distinctive facade with the large recessed niche cut into the blocky, almost square facade topped by a pyramidal roof. The niche is plastic and sculptural, carved into rather than added, as is common with much of the other architectural detail of the Lawn. Seen at night it stands out. The four windows appear diminutive in comparison with those of the other pavilions. In contrast to most of the other pavilions, the Tuscan colonnade marches right across, and it lacks a giant order. This facade has been likened to several sources, most notably the Parisian Hotel de Guimard, designed by Claude-Nicholas Ledoux in 1770. Jefferson, the speculation goes, must have seen it while in Paris as the American ambassador between 1784 and 1789. However, Jefferson neither mentioned it nor showed any interest in the "modern" or "revolutionary" architecture that Ledoux represented. More likely, Benjamin Henry

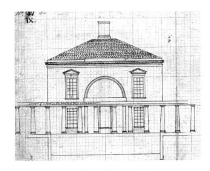

Study for Pavilion IX, c. 29 March 1819, Thomas Jefferson

Latrobe suggested the facade back in mid-1817, and Jefferson adapted it. Jefferson inscribed on the drawing, and on the rear, "Latrobe." Such niches or exedrae are not uncommon; Latrobe used them in his own work, and Jefferson would have noted them in the various books he owned. Indeed, as the ultimate source of such a niche is ancient Roman, that alone would have recommended it to Jefferson.

Jefferson's original specifications called for the Tuscan order from Palladio, but he changed during construction to the Ionic of Temple of Fortuna Virilis from Palladio, and two one-story Ionic columns flank the door. Master joiner John Neilson, carpenter Carter, brickmason William Phillips, and builder George Wilson Spooner carried out construction. The first resident was George Tucker, a 44-years-old lawyer and essay writer. Hired to teach moral philosophy, Tucker remained at the University for 20 years. His successor in 1845, the Reverend William Holmes McGuffy, was the author of the famous "McGuffy Reader" or the *Eclectic Readers*, which taught generations of children in the nineteenth century to read. He was also a Presbyterian minister, and the first cleric hired to the University's faculty.

10. Pavilion X *Thomas Jefferson, 1819–1822*

Among the last pavilions to go up, Pavilion X was built under the direction of master joiner John Neilson and brickmason William Phillips. Jefferson designed it in June 1819 and specified Doric of Theater of Marcellus from Chambray as the source for the orders and entablature. Instead of the usual Roman Doric order with a molded base, or a torus, Jefferson specified no base, making a tentative gesture toward the Greek. A square three-inch-thick plinth provides a footing for the columns. Proportionally, the columns resemble the elongated profile of Roman Doric and lack the stoutness of the Greek Doric.

Jefferson's drawing for Pavilion X shows a parapet that hides the roof. His source came from the Temple of Nerva Trajan, which he had also used at Monticello for the parapet there. One can surmise that constructed of wood the parapet had problems, perhaps with drainage during rain, because about 1870 it was removed and never replaced. Jefferson experimented with roofing schemes at the University, including a type of tin shingle. For a variety of reasons, weathered shingles were never replaced and instead other roofing

Study for Pavilion X, June 1819, Thomas Jefferson

materials were substituted. Pavilion X's roof has been restored and displays Jefferson's original tin roofing.

The facade features complicated ornamentation. The frieze has the traditional triglyphs, blank metopes, and dentil molding of the Doric, which appears simple against the elaborate cornice. The cornice adapted from the Theater of Marcellus is fully on display, with the soffit of rectangular guttae blocks and rosettes of four petals, made of lead. At the corners, eight-petaled rosettes heighten the effect of large medallions.

The first residents, Dr. Robley Dunglison and his bride, arrived in February 1825. A native of Scotland, Dunglison's degrees in medicine from England and Germany, a diploma from the Society of Apothecaries, and his writings on medical subjects made him very attractive to Jefferson. He became the first full-time professor of medicine at an American university. Immediately after his arrival, he informed Jefferson that his front room was not the appropriate location for dissections and the teaching of anatomy and requested a new building. Jefferson responded with the design of the Anatomical Theatre. Dunglison attended Jefferson during his last year, and was at his bedside when he died on July 4, 1826.

Pavilion X

11. Rotunda *Thomas Jefferson, 1822–1826*

The Rotunda was the last of the major buildings to be erected. It had a large force of workers, including John Dinsmore and John Neilson as joiners, William Phillips as master brickmason, John Perry, and others who worked on the structure between October 1822, when foundation work began, and September 1826, its completion. Jefferson valued the Rotunda so highly that he refused to open the University until its construction was well advanced. Its purpose was to house the library in the dome, and on the floors below to provide classrooms and spaces for meetings.

The design and the meanings associated with it derive from complicated origins. Latrobe first proposed a domed form in his letter to Jefferson of July 24, 1817. Apparently Latrobe sent other drawings that have since been lost. Jefferson initially acknowledged Latrobe's contribution by including his name on the front of the elevation drawing and then crossing it out, then placing Latrobe's name on the rear and subsequently erasing it. Why Jefferson removed Latrobe's name remains unclear, but the most probable reason is that Latrobe was in serious trouble with President

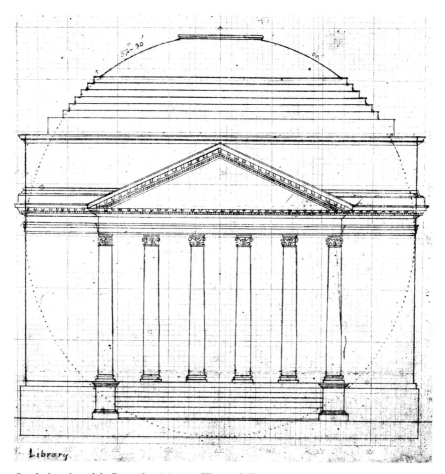

South elevation of the Rotunda, 1818–1819, Thomas Jefferson

James Monroe over faulty construction the US Capitol; indeed within a few months, his employment would be terminated. As a member of the Board of Visitors, Monroe might have objected to Latrobe's involvement. Jefferson adopted Latrobe's suggestion, but turned to his own edition of Leoni's *Architecture of A. Palladio* for specific sources.

Jefferson explained the adoption on the rear of one of the drawings: "[Latrobe's —erased] Rotunda, reduced to the proportions of the pantheon and accommodated to the purposes of a Library for the University with the rooms for drawing, music, examinations and other accessory purposes. The diameter of the building 77 feet, being 1/2 of the Pantheon, consequently 1/4 A, area, H 1/8 volume." However, a comparison reveals substantial differences between the Pantheon in Rome and as Jefferson once called the Rotunda, the "Pantheon" in Charlottesville. The Pantheon has an octastyle portico at ground level, while the Rotunda has a six-columned portico reached by an imposing staircase. And Jefferson's portico is tied into the composition and not simply appended, as in Rome. The internal spatial organization of the Rotunda differs significantly from the Pantheon.

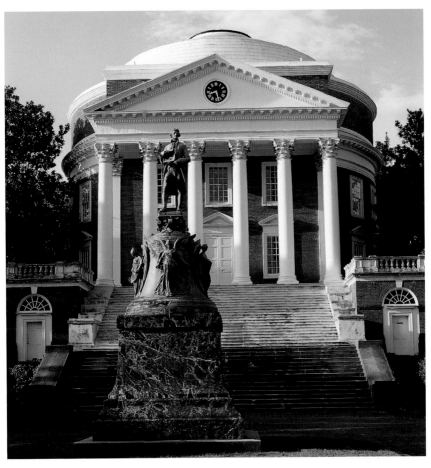

Rotunda

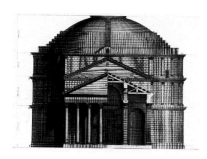

Giacomo Leoni, Architecture of
A. Palladio: In Four Books, 3rd edition
(London, 1742), Book IV, Chapter XX,
Plates LVI and LVII, Special Collections
Department, Rare Books Division,
University of Virginia Library

Jefferson considered the Pantheon a "perfect example" of spherical architecture. It had the approbation of the ancients. Jefferson admired domes; he added one to Monticello and suggested a cylindrical structure with a dome for his design for the US Capitol circa 1791. With the University's Rotunda he took a shape that in pagan religions stood for the cosmos, and then in Christianity came to represent the heavens, and worked it into a temple of reason, or the storehouse of knowledge. One of Jefferson's great contributions lay in making the library the central building of the modern university.

The original Rotunda was built of brick and wood. Jefferson derived the dome's wooden truss system from a French architect, Philibert Delorme. On either side of the south-facing grand staircase, brick terraces linked the structure to the pavilions and dormitories. The space beneath the terraces served initially as a gymnasium, and later filled other purposes. The fire of October 1895, which largely destroyed the Rotunda and Robert Mills's Annex brought Stanford White onto the scene as the reconstruction architect. Actually, White replaced a Louisville, Kentucky, architect, Harry McDonald, who was in Charlottesville supervising the construction of the new Christ Episcopal Church downtown. The Board of Visitors enlisted McDonald immediately after the fire, no doubt because was convenient and at hand. But McDonald's plans for a cast-iron interior met with opposition, and when one of the remaining brick walls of the Rotunda—which he claimed were sound and did not need to be rebuilt—collapsed, McDonald was terminated and White hired. At the direction of the University's rector and some faculty, White added a new north portico, and extended the terraces around the structure to link up the two sides. This elevated walk affords a dramatic view of the University and the Lawn, while underneath space is devoted to offices. White based the new north portico on Jefferson's south portico, intending it to be the new entrance to the University. The visitor would climb the steps and enter the Rotunda into a vast two-story space, the library, with books covering the walls. Leaving the building, the visitor would be greeted by the pavilions and colonnades stretching out to the southwest. White explained his decision on the Rotunda's interior as "a nearer approach to a classic and ideal treatment," which "Jefferson would unquestionably have adopted himself had he been able to do so when the Rotunda was built." Essentially, White argued, Jefferson for a number of reasons really could not build an interior similar to the Pantheon, but he, White, knew that was what

Jefferson had wanted, and he would accomplish it.

By the 1930s the inherent problems of a circular library, which had plagued Jefferson's original, had again surfaced, and Alderman Library was constructed. This left the Rotunda with no purpose other than social and honorary. Between 1973 and 1976, a team of architects and historians, including Ballou and Justice of Richmond with Frederick Doveton Nichols, architectural history professor at the University, as adviser. removed the Stanford White interior and installed a facsimile of Jefferson's. They kept Stanford White's dome, which closely copied Jefferson's, however, he employed Guastavino vaulting, a clay tile system, very strong and, of course, fireproof. The restoration returned Jefferson's original spaces and made some attempt at duplicating the original trim; however, since no detailed drawings remained from Jefferson's time, the architects had to rely on educated guesses. On the basement level three oval rooms flank the hourglass-shaped entrance hall. The basement east oval room that origi-nally housed a chemistry laboratory now serves as a museum for the his-tory of the Lawn. The basement's west oval and north oval rooms were likely classrooms, and today serve as lecture and reception spaces. Twin staircases lead to the main floor, with the vast luminous and curving hall. The cornice that surrounds the space and lends emphasis to the undulating walls is a plain Tuscan order. The life-size statue of Jefferson, sculpted by Alexander Galt in 1860 originally stood on the library floor overhead; stu-dents saved it from the fire of 1895. The main floor's east oval room origi-nally served as a classroom; today, as the grand table suggests, it is a meeting room for the Board of Visitors. The cornice is Corinthian from the Baths of Caracalla. A portrait of Jefferson by Bass Otis hangs over the man-tel, which is modeled on a mantel found in the pavilions. The main-floor west oval room, also originally a classroom, features fine Federal style fur-niture and serves as a reception room. The entablature is Doric from the Baths of Diocletian. A Thomas Sully life portrait of Jefferson hangs over the mantel. The main floor's north oval room, a classroom, is bordered by an Ionic frieze copied from the Temple of Fortune Virilis in Rome, according to Palladio; it now houses meetings and examinations.

The dome room that occupies the top level and originally served as the library offers a wonderful example of a neoclassical space with its low curve, a part of a perfect sphere. The acoustical paneling on the dome's inner surface is obviously not original and therefore mars the impact. Equally troubling is the modern skylight, which clashes. Jefferson's skylight, regrettably, leaked, generating a variety of attempted solutions over the years. Never carried out but suggested by Jefferson was to paint the inte-rior of the dome a dark blue, and he devised a complicated system for pro-jecting the heavens on its surface. The dome would function as a planetarium, reinforcing the idea of a temple of the Enlightenment. Around the room Jefferson arranged a gallery carried on twenty pairs of composite columns. This order in a sense completed the display of all five classical orders in the Rotunda. The reconstruction of the 1970s substituted plaster capitals for Jefferson's original specification of black locust. Modern safety codes demand steel railings. The room hosts lectures and social functions. The first social function occurred November 5, 1824, when the University hosted a gala banquet for the Marquis de Lafayette, with 400 seated male guests. Women were placed on the lawn. Near the conclusion of the dinner, master builder James Dinsmore, who had worked on the Rotunda, arose and offered a toast, which is repeated after most University banquets: "Thomas Jefferson, founder of the University of Virginia."

12. West Pavilion Gardens

Thomas Jefferson's love of gardening is legendary. In 1814, after retiring from the presidency, he wrote, "No occupation is so delightful to me as the culture of the earth, and no culture comparable to that of the garden. I am still devoted to the garden. But though an old man, I am but a young gardener." Recognizing the importance of such matters to the rural economy of state and nation, he exhibited a lively interest in the scientific aspects of horticulture and its application to fruit and vegetable culture, having once declared, "The greatest service which can be rendered any country is to add a useful plant to its culture." He also recognized the deeper meaning of gardens within the cultural traditions of Western civilization. Indeed he argued that gardening, which he described as "embellishing grounds by fancy," should rank among the fine arts.

Perhaps there is no better demonstration of Jefferson's skillful integration of architecture and landscape than the plan for the Academical Village, in which each professor is given a dwelling overlooking an adjacent garden space. This union of house and garden traces its roots to the rural villas of classical antiquity, described in the writings of Horace and Pliny that Jefferson knew so well. The pavilion gardens, integral to the architectural framework of the institution as the link between Lawn and Range, have remained a unique feature of the University grounds. In 1908, noted Boston landscape architect Warren Manning observed: "One of the most attractive features of the original plan and an indication of the refinements of that day which we have yet to attain, was the provision for gardens at each residence hall." Today, these quiet enclaves balance the more active open space of the Lawn, inviting contemplation and refreshment of spirit.

Although the gardens figure importantly in the original plan of the Academical Village, no Jeffersonian plans survive to indicate the nature of the interior plantings. Jefferson probably intended the spaces as the private domestic domain of the professors living on the Lawn, who would shape them to meet their needs. It does appear, however, that Jefferson thought of them as pleasure gardens since he took great care to distinguish "yards" from "gardens" in his planning. Following typical practice of the period, the yards were the shared outdoor areas to the north and south of each pavilion. Now parking lots, these areas accommodated the cisterns, woodpiles and other service functions of the adjacent households. Straight walls enclosed the yards, in contrast to the serpentine walls framing the garden spaces. Although the serpentine walls were not a Jeffersonian invention, he used them here to such fine aesthetic effect that they have become one of the signature design features of the University.

Over the years, the pavilion residents wrought many changes to the garden spaces, tearing down walls and putting up sheds, kitchens, stables, and other outbuildings. Over time, these alterations eroded the purity of the original design. In 1948, the Garden Club of Virginia responded to the University's request for assistance by hiring Alden Hopkins, the resident landscape architect at Colonial Williamsburg, to develop a master plan for refurbishing the ten gardens. With proceeds from Historic Garden Week tours, the Garden Club funded construction of the West Lawn Gardens, which were dedicated in 1952. Based on archaeological investigations and the engravings of the University plan by Peter Maverick in 1822 and 1825, which are believed to represent the actual condition of the University during Jefferson's lifetime, the garden walls were reconstructed in their earliest

Pavilion III garden, detail of original capital

configuration. Although all the gardens contained privies, only two sets have been rebuilt in Gardens I and IX, where they serve as storage sheds today.

The Colonial Revival style of garden design developed in the 1930s at Colonial Williamsburg guided the layout of the West Lawn Gardens. In the absence of solid documentation for the original configuration of the gardens, the designer drew upon a lexicon of forms and materials derived from better documented gardens of the same period as well as descriptions from contemporary garden literature. These precedents molded new designs that were compatible with the architecture of the period. Colonial Revival gardens were never intended to duplicate the gardens' historical appearance. They are twentieth-century gardens designed to meet contemporary needs, the artistic creations of very accomplished landscape architects that value aesthetic quality over historical accuracy.

In the design of the West Range gardens, Hopkins drew on Jefferson's own writing about horticulture in general and his gardens at Monticello in particular. Edwin Betts's *Jefferson's Garden Book* (1944), inspired the plant selections. In general, the plant palette draws from varieties that date to the early nineteenth century, a time when many new plants were introduced to the nursery following the botanical explorations of the Orient and western North America. Each of the five gardens is different, in the layout of paths and planting beds as well as the design of gates and benches, which are unique to each garden setting. The styles within the gardens epitomize the transition in garden design during Jefferson's lifetime. In eighteenth-century England, "landscape gardens," with paths curving through sweeping lawns and clumps of trees, replaced the traditional gardens of geometrically arranged flowerbeds, called parterres. Jefferson avidly tracked these trends, visiting fashionable English and European gardens while he was Minister to France.

The gardens reflect the changing tastes in garden design. The curving path of Pavilion III meanders through planting beds filled with perennials and shrubs in a manner adapted from the English landscape garden. George Washington's garden at Mount Vernon and Jefferson's own roundabout flower walk at Monticello serve as direct American precedents for the design. The upper garden of Pavilion V models the "old style" garden of geometric parterres edged in trimmed boxwood. The three gardens behind Pavilions I, V, and IX, are divided by serpentine cross walls in Jefferson's plans because they were to be shared by hotels on the Range. In each case, the lower garden is simpler than the corresponding upper garden, planted in fruit trees and other edible varieties. Gardens I and III highlight artifacts from the early years of the University's construction, when Jefferson was experimenting with carving local stone. The results of these failed experiments now play an admirable role as garden ornaments, forming a touchstone connecting past and present.

West Range

13. West Range *Thomas Jefferson, 1820–1822*

Many visitors to the Lawn pass by the ranges very swiftly, treating them as
a minor prelude to the great event beyond. However, not only did Jefferson
design them; they demonstrate the scope of his architectural expression.
Spatially, they offer a completely different experience, the long run of
arcade creating a different frame from the landscape beyond. The West
Range fronts on McCormick Road and the terrain here is a gentle grade,
unlike the East Range. Jefferson designed the West Range around 1819, and
brickmason and illustrator John Neilson later made drawings of the hotels.
The West Range, comprising Hotels, A, C, and E, and 26 dormitory rooms,
was constructed between 1820 and 1822. The dormitory rooms are identical
to those on the Lawn, and one room, No. 13, is restored as a memorial to
Edgar Allan Poe; visitors can view it through a glass partition.

Jefferson intended that the hotels in the ranges would provide dining for students and faculty. Students would sign up for, or be assigned to,
a hotel run by a hotelkeeper approved by the University. Jefferson envisioned scholars eating at a common table and discussing intellectual subjects, even conversing in foreign languages at meals. The idea was sound,
but problems arose not just with students but with getting qualified hotelkeepers. Low student enrollment also created financial hardships for the
hotelkeepers, and many did not last long.

At the north end, Hotel A has two entrances, one from the arcade
and one on the north facade, a stout Doric portico. This portico is original

and figures in both a drawing by John Neilson and the Maverick Plan. To the rear of Hotel A, in the garden of Pavilion I, stood a large brick structure that also served as a refectory for students and faculty. It has been demolished. Hotel A later housed a physiology laboratory, and since 1928 the editorial offices of the *Virginia Quarterly Review* have occupied it. The west front arcade steps forward with slightly wider arches to denote the hierarchy of the hotels.

Hotel C, in the middle of the range, is fronted by a five-bayed arcaded porch. Nicknamed "Jeff Hall," its major occupant is the Jefferson Debating Society, founded July 14, 1825. The low initial student enrollment meant that not all the hotels were needed for eating, and Hotel C very early housed a student social center for dances and meetings. In the mid-nineteenth century, fencing lessons took place here. Later in the nineteenth century, the Jefferson Debating Society and the Raven Society (an honorary for students and faculty) took up residence. The structure is arranged as an early classroom with a raised dais and numerous old portraits on the walls. The basement spaces were originally planned for dining and a kitchen.

Hotel E, at the far south end, was originally subleased from the University by John Gray Jr., who contracted to provide food for the students. However, Gray enjoyed drinking and gambling with the students too much and the University authorities forced him out after two years, though they allowed his wife, Mrs. Gray, who was the sister of Proctor Brockenbrough, to remain. Known as "Mrs. Gray's hotel," the building operated for more than 20 years under her stewardship. In 1858 a two-story annex to the south was added to provide more student dining space. After the turn of the century, Hotel E became faculty residences, and in 1919 the large upstairs room in the addition became the first school of architecture under Fiske Kimball. The hotel subsequently served other purposes, and then it again became a dining facility, this time for the adjacent Colonnade Club in Pavilion VII.

14. East Pavilion Gardens

The history of the East Lawn Gardens parallels that of the West Lawn Gardens, although the steeper topography on the east results in gardens of a different size and character. Following the successful dedication of the West Lawn Gardens in 1952, the Garden Club of Virginia proceeded with plans to refurbish walls and gardens on the east. Moving a major service road that passed through the middle of the original Jeffersonian enclosures complicated the project with unforeseen costs. The trace of this road can be discerned in the narrow middle terrace of the gardens today.

Serpentine wall

The Garden Club again retained Alden Hopkins to design the gardens. After Hopkins's sudden death, the commission fell to Donald H. Parker, Hopkins's assistant at Colonial Williamsburg, and Ralph E. Griswold, a noted landscape architect from Pittsburgh. Dedicated in 1965, the gardens exemplify the Colonial Revival style established by Hopkins in the West Lawn Gardens.

Archaeological investigations uncovered sections of original serpentine walls, as well as evidence of various outbuildings from later eras. The Maverick engravings of 1822 and 1825 show that all ten gardens initially had privies set into the walls on the north and south sides of the gardens. The 1960s wall reconstruction rebuilt only three sets of privies. These now function as tool sheds, while the footprints of the others are marked by brick outlines on the ground plane.

Serpentine walls enclose the garden; straight wall sections define the work areas, or "yards." In Gardens II, VI, and VIII, cross walls also separate upper gardens from lower gardens, used by the hotel keepers of the corresponding dining halls on the Range. While the undulating walls heighten the charm of the gardens and alleyways, Jefferson also had practical

Pavilion VI garden

reasons for using the serpentine form. He carefully calculated that this type of construction would require fewer bricks than the traditional straight wall, which must be two bricks thick to maintain its structural stability.

As on the West Lawn, the plantings reflect the contrast between the prevailing fashions in garden design during the eighteenth and early-nineteenth centuries, juxtaposing geometric planting beds with curvilinear paths and roundabout walks. The upper garden of Pavilion IV retains the boxwood garden of Maximilian Schele de Vere, professor of modern languages, an avid gardener who lived here from 1845–97. The lower garden of Pavilion VI next door derives its inspiration as a "wilderness garden" from the white pine and Norway spruce shading the site. Jefferson's notes about the "small thickets of shrubs" he particularly admired at Blenheim Castle during his 1786 English garden tour inspired the plantings of native shrubs and wildflowers. The focal point is one of the fifteenth-century spires from Merton College Chapel in England.

15. East Range   *Thomas Jefferson, 1820–1822*

The prospect of the East Range is very different from that of the West; the incline of the ridge is steeper and consequently, Jefferson placed the structures farther from the Lawn. Located along a partially man-made terrace, the East Range buildings overlook a small valley that now cradles the Medical Center complex. Architecturally, the East Range resembles the West Range: long deep runs of arcades front the twenty-six dormitory rooms, and three hotels, B, D and F, rise above them. The arcades step forward in front of the hotels and are noticeably higher and larger. The various sections of the East Range were constructed between 1820 and 1822 with brickmasons John Perry, William Phillips, and George Spooner among the most prominent builders. The dormitory rooms are still occupied by students, and the hotels now serve administrative functions.

Hotel B at the northern end was the only building other than the Anatomical Theater to have a square plan. Jefferson's drawing shows it as 34 feet by 34 feet. But a revised plan, lacking the arcade added two bays at the north end. The hotel rises up higher than the arcade in front and displays the Tuscan order. The small Ionic columned portico and window pediments on Hotel B's north face are clearly Victorian, and were added about 1869, when the building was occupied by the Washington Debating Society.

The middle hotel, D, was first designed by Jefferson to be 34 feet wide, but he increased it to the present 50 feet. Five arches front the hotel on the east, and it also has an alley entry to the rear with a fanlight over the door. The commodious first floor, with three rooms and a central hall, never served as a dining hall, and Arthur S. Brockenbrough, the proctor, who

East Range

supervised construction from 1819 onward, moved in. Later it became a fencing academy, and also served as a center for student dances.

      The last East Range hotel occupying the south end, F, is the only two-story, pedimented hotel on the ranges. Both Jefferson's original drawing and the elevation today show strong similarities to his first 1814 pavilion scheme for the Albemarle Academy. Both called for three bays with a central entrance and a lunette in the pediment. The floor plans were nearly identical, with only a slight change in the staircase. The stout Tuscan-order arcade replaced the 1814 colonnade of piers. The original occupant, James Byers, a hotelkeeper, stayed only four months and was succeeded by J. B. Richeson. Within a year, S. B. Chapman had taken over. The problem, again, lay in a lack of student borders. In 1857, with a two-story addition to the south, Hotel F became the University's first gymnasium. Its crenellated brick cornice contrasts with the Tuscan order of the original hotel. Another addition on the second floor to the north was made in 1890. To the rear stands the "cracker box," a two-story brick building that served as kitchen and cook's quarters; today it is student housing.

Central Grounds

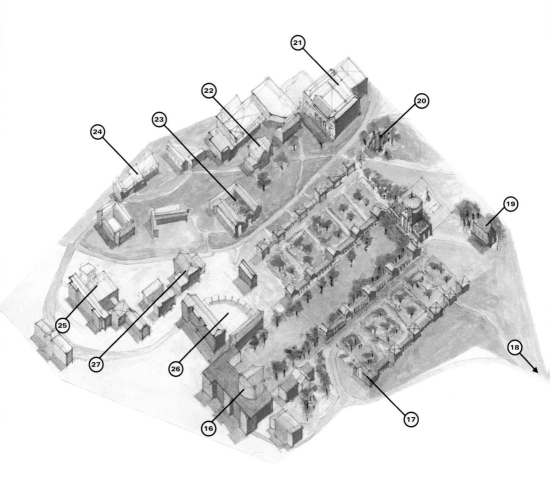

Expanding the Academical Village

The Central Grounds walk visits the buildings and landscapes that encircle the Academical Village. The area, like the Jefferson complex that spawned it but unlike the University's later automobile-dependent grounds, remains pedestrian. Despite the variety of functions housed in the structures originally, most are now academic buildings. Because the earliest additions to the University clung to the outskirts of the Jefferson complex, this walk includes the University's largest collection of buildings from the Romantic Picturesque village era of the mid nineteenth century. Varsity Hall, Brooks Hall, the University Chapel, and Dawson's Row happily defied the Jefferson memory to revel in variety, only to draw scorn later. The Rotunda fire in 1895 brought an end to the parade of architectural styles.

Cocke, Cabell, and Rouss Halls at the south end of the Lawn, designed by McKim, Mead & White, America's most prominent architectural firm at the turn of the twentieth century, sowed the seeds that matured into a cohesive University style. Imposing Jefferson Revival buildings, arranged to frame outdoor courts, presented the ideal, if not the fact, of University architecture until the 1960s. The eclectic, earliest buildings of the Central Grounds, such as Varsity Hall and Dawson's Row, ignored the siting of the Academical Village. By comparison, the designers who returned to Jefferson produced not only individual buildings that looked to the work of the founder but also two notable but very different complexes—the grand court fronting Alderman Library and the more intimate collection centered on the McIntire Amphitheater.

In the 1920s, the University Architectural Commission picked up the McKim, Mead & White mantle. Its work, the buildings of Mr. Alderman's University, dots the area. The Monroe Hill dormitories, at that time the University's largest dormitory complex, revolutionized—although not without anguish and controversy—student housing at the University. Monroe Hall housed the social science programs that trained agents who were central to fabricating the New South. Clark Hall, built as the stately home of the Law School, capped a prominent site and stood at the gateway to the University's post-World War II expansion. The Jefferson legacy, which weighed heavily on the buildings in the Central Grounds walk, fueled the lively dialogue between old and new.

Over time, some of the fragments of the old University disappeared as the evolving University claimed a number of architectural victims. Jefferson's Anatomical Theater was demolished in the wake of a more radical change, the removal of a library as the focal point of the Lawn. The light sprinkling of early residential buildings around the Academical Village gave way to bulky institutional structures. Dawson's Row, despite the gloss of colonial porticoes applied early in the twentieth century, vanished to make room for the larger academic buildings that the growing university demanded. The house of J. W. Mallet, the chemistry professor who built Miller Hall, formerly occupied the site of Monroe Hall. Today, Miller Hall is also slated for demolition to provide more room for the ever-expanding library. The transience and expendability of the buildings in the orbit contrast sharply with the seeming permanence of those at the center. At the core, physically and psychologically, lies the Academical Village, the soul of the University and its most sacred relic, still inhabited today and wrapped in the protective blanket of the buildings and landscapes of the Central Grounds walk.

16. Cocke Hall, Cabell Hall, and Rouss Hall

Stanford White of McKim, Mead & White, 1896–1898

In one sense, the construction of Cocke, Cabell, and Rouss Halls at the south end of the Lawn simply offered a physical answer to a functional problem that had been ignited by the Rotunda fire. The Rotunda Annex had contained classrooms and a public assembly hall. The 1895 fire destroyed the University's only large gathering hall and obliterated a significant portion of its indispensable academic space. This set of buildings, designed by Stanford White of the prominent New York firm McKim, Mead & White, replaced these lost facilities. Cabell Hall, the new Academical Building, housed an auditorium. Like Cabell Hall, Cocke and Rouss Halls also contained replacement classrooms.

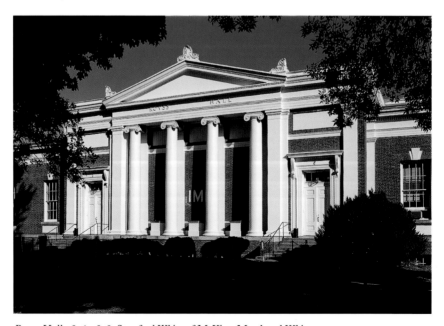

Rouss Hall, 1896–1898, Stanford White of McKim, Mead and White

Cabell Hall, interior, auditorium

Nonetheless, White's complex provided more than just a utilitarian solution to an immediate physical need. There were also ideological implications embedded in the design of the new buildings. With the construction of the large warehouses, honeycombed with classroom cells, the University cemented a commitment to a building type. The forms of the three buildings—each a rectangular block containing multiple classrooms—differed radically from the files of discrete pavilions in the Jefferson plan, but they were not unprecedented at the University. The McKim, Mead & White buildings did not insolently diverge from the prevailing pattern but rather quietly echoed the organization of Robert Mills's destroyed Rotunda Annex. The new structures codified the form that future growth at the University would take—sealing, not initiating, a decision that had, in fact, already been made.

Although the new complex of buildings ably answered the pressing need for academic facilities, the transformation of the campus was dramatic. The intended primary approach to the Academical Village had been from the south. White has often been blamed for the siting of the buildings, which closed the south end of the Lawn, but it was the Board of Visitors that actually selected that alternative. The controversial closing of the vista and the rebuilding of the Rotunda relocated the principal campus entry to the north, through or around the Rotunda, and discreetly blocked the view of an adjacent, largely African-American community, which contemporaries found unsightly.

While the placement of Cabell Hall has prompted endless debate, White's buildings deferred to the Academical Village. The familiar vocabulary of red brick and white trim tied the new works visually to the Jefferson buildings. The subdivision of the long façade, which reads as a central pavilion with flanking wings, diminished its apparent size. Treating each entry as a pavilion harmonized the new work with the buildings of the Jefferson complex. Terracing the sloping site neatly solved the potential problem of inserting a building whose size far exceeded that of the Rotunda. By setting the ground-floor elevation of the buildings at twenty feet below the bottom step of the Rotunda, the architects trimmed the apparent height of the new structures. If the McKim, Mead & White connection to Jefferson was tenuous, their impact on later building at the University was not. Their design was the point of departure for subsequent work in the University Beautiful period of the early twentieth century.

As the building that terminates the axis of the Lawn, Cabell Hall was detailed to reinforce its prominence relative to the others in the group. Unlike those of Cocke and Rouss, Cabell's pavilion projects forward from the plane of the building to form a sheltering portico over the central entry. Unlike the other two, the pediment of Cabell Hall contains an elaborate sculptural group by George Julian Zolnay. The theme is an allegory based on the Greek motto inscribed in the frieze, "Ye Shall Know the Truth and the Truth Shall Make You Free." Despite the high-mindedness of the theme, Zolnay's models for the pediment figures were, ironically, not classical prototypes but instead were, as Anna Barringer notes, employees from "the most respectable bordello in town." George W. Breck's copy of Raphael's *School of Athens*, installed in 1902 on the north wall of the auditorium, replaced the University's earlier *School of Athens* copy, which had been lost in the burning of the Rotunda Annex.

The building names commemorated luminaries from the University's past as well as contemporary benefactors. The Mechanical Laboratory, now known as Cocke Hall, honored John Hartwell Cocke, owner of nearby Bremo, a friend of Jefferson's, and a member of the original Board of Visitors. Cabell Hall, originally called the Academical Building, honored Joseph C. Cabell, an early rector of the University. Rouss Hall, the Physical Laboratory, memorialized the building's principal donor, Charles Broadway Rouss, a wealthy New York City merchant who was the son of a nearby valley farmer. In the early 1950s Eggers and Higgins enlarged Cabell Hall with a substantial addition to the south, named New Cabell Hall. To the east is Wilson Hall, designed by Johnson, Craven and Gibson, which opened in 1969. The structure provided additional room when New Cabell Hall too had been outgrown. Although departments have come and gone from the structures, each remains a classroom and office building.

Nearby sculpture, commissioned later, contributed to the commemorative wash applied to the grounds during the Alderman years. Moses Ezekiel's 1907 group, which depicts Homer with his young guide, stands at the center of the grand forecourt. Two other works occupy the deferential buffer zone between the McKim, Mead & White work and the Jefferson buildings. On the east, a replica of the Houdon Washington, which had been commissioned by Jefferson for the Virginia State Capitol, was the gift of a University graduate, John T. Lupton of Chattanooga, Tennessee. On the west, Karl Bitter's seated Jefferson, like the Senff Gates, was dedicated on Founder's Day 1915, only a few days after Bitter's untimely death. The three works, which celebrated the arts, education, and two framers of American democracy, also promoted the University as a caretaker of cultural memory.

Varsity Hall *1857–1858*
Randall Hall *1898–1899, Paul Pelz*

Varsity Hall, 1857–1858

Standing side by side, Varsity and Randall Halls neatly encapsulate the changes in architecture at the University between the mid and late nineteenth century. Varsity Hall's Italianate detailing and its siting, askew from the Academical Village, characterize the picturesque architecture at mid century. By contrast, Randall Hall, brimming with classical detailing, follows the McKim, Mead & White plan.

Varsity Hall, the original University infirmary, built twenty years after the completion of the Academical Village, reversed the University's policy toward illness. Jefferson saw the typical academic building of his day as a "large and common den of noise, of filth, and of fetid air." His approach to illness aimed at prevention rather than treatment. He dispersed separate functions to individual buildings in an effort to thwart the spread of contagious diseases. Despite his efforts, diseases regularly ravaged his Academical Village. A series of epidemics in the mid-nineteenth century prompted the Board of Visitors to allocate money for an infirmary in 1857. The structure is one of the earliest surviving non-Jeffersonian buildings on the grounds.

The infirmary actively promoted separation. Pushed away from the Academical Village in order to quarantine the sick, the building also did not take its orientation from the Jefferson plan. Similarly, the style, fashionable by mid-century, rejected the founder's vocabulary. Bracketed cornices mimicked at Varsity Hall by corbelled brickwork, and the slender vertical windows are hallmarks of the Italianate style.

The Randall Building began as a 43-room dormitory. In 1872, the Board of Visitors enacted a policy that required students to live in University housing. The desire to house the students on the grounds and the growing enrollments in the late nineteenth century fed the demand for additional dormitory space outside of the Academical Village. With the addition of the Monroe Hill dormitories in 1848, Dawson's Row about 1859, and the Carr's Hill dormitories after 1867, the University acted to house its increasing student population. Randall Hall was another link in this chain. An 1898 gift from the J. W. and Belinda Randall estate provided the funding for the new dormitories.

Randall Hall

While Randall Hall's appearance diverges from that of most of its predecessors, it also differs from the architecture built in the early 1900s. A post-McKim, Mead & White product, the building is laden with classical detailing. On the facade, cartouches above the first-floor windows bear the monograms of the building's donors. The pedimented gables, rich moldings, and Ionic columns *in antis* that flank the entry are a heavy classical overlay on a building with mixed ancestry. The complex massing, polychromatic flat arches, as well as the profusion of applied ornamentation sprang from Victorian roots. Randall Hall was designed by prominent Washington, DC, architect Paul Pelz, whose most well-known work, the Library of Congress building, had been completed only the year before, in 1897. With the growing appreciation of the architectural significance of the Jefferson complex at the turn of the century, the University sought out well-known architects, whose reputations matched its perception of the stature of the Grounds.

Both Varsity and Randall Halls today house new functions. After the completion of Pelz's hospital in the early 1900s, the infirmary was redundant. Later used successively as a fraternity house, dormitory, and residence, the building was renamed Varsity Hall in 1919, when the nurses moved next door to Randall Hall. Since the 1950s Varsity Hall has housed the Air Force ROTC program. Randall Hall remained a dormitory into the 1950s. Today it houses the Corcoran Department of History.

18. Senff Gates   *Henry Bacon, 1914–1915*

The Senff Gates, which frame the eastern entrance, were one component of the comprehensive yet gentle manipulation of the University landscape in the early twentieth century, through the overlay of commemorative objects. Progressive President Alderman transformed the University not only by redirecting its mission but also by reworking the physical fabric of the Grounds. Two of the projects he promoted, Henry Bacon's Senff Gates and Karl Bitter's seated Jefferson, were dedicated on Founder's Day in 1915. Mrs. Charles H. Senff funded the brick and marble gates as a memorial to her husband, a University graduate and benefactor, and as a celebration of the University's honor system. A slate tablet records the gift.

The embellishment of the east entrance, was one offshoot of the awakened interest in the formal composition of the grounds. To direct his

Senff Gates, 1914–1915, Henry Bacon

expansion of Jefferson's university, Alderman, in good Progressive fashion, sought out an expert. In 1908, he engaged landscape architect Warren Manning of Boston to guide the University building committee. He also commissioned a master plan to order the growth of the institution. The program for Eugene Bradbury's neo-Jeffersonian Corner Building originally included the gates. Alderman suggested a redesign of Bradbury's gates, and Manning recommended Henry Bacon as the architect.

Local and national forces influenced the design of the Senff Gates. Bacon was at the crest of his fame; his most well-known work, the Lincoln Memorial, was underway when he took on the University commission in 1914. Formal masonry gates sprang up at a number of other university entrances in the early twentieth century. Charles McKim's 1901 Class of 1877 gate at Harvard spawned a number of imitators, including the Senff Gates. The gates are a Jefferson-Georgian conflation, inspired by cultural and aesthetic ambitions that paralleled those of the City Beautiful designers. A reinterpretation of the Jefferson vocabulary, the grander brick and marble gates replaced the earlier wooden fence and gate that had marked the boundaries of the University. In the days before automobiles and suburbanization, the continuous enclosure had kept both large, grazing animals and unwanted traffic out of the grounds. Bacon recast the physical barrier as a sophisticated symbolic entrance.

Decades before, in the early nineteenth century, professors' gardens occupied the triangle of land west of the Senff Gates. The closing of the south end of the Lawn and the acknowledgment of the growing use of University Avenue as a traffic artery emphasized the importance of the entrances at the north end of the Grounds. The Senff Gates are the entrance to the grounds along University Avenue, marking the main vehicular entrance to the University from Charlottesville.

19. Brooks Hall   *John Rochester Thomas, 1876–1877*

Brooks Hall, completed in 1877 and opened in 1878 as a museum of natural science, embodied a central preoccupation of the period, the interest in science in the post-Darwin world. A monument to evolution, Brooks Hall was built nearly a half century before the Scopes trial put evolution itself on trial. The structure housed the University's first museum, which was pointedly dedicated to science rather than art. Although the building type was new to the University, natural science collections were not unprecedented, even in the early nineteenth century. Jefferson's artifacts displayed in the front hall of Monticello testify to his interest in natural history. Yet a large systematically organized collection, such as that displayed in the Brooks Museum, was rare until the post-Civil War period. The University museum's spacious interior housed thousands of specimens, assembled and organized to illustrate the process of evolution.

The exterior of Brooks Hall displayed carved animal heads ornamenting the keystones of the arches above the openings, and the names of prominent natural historians ringed the building. In the manner of

Brooks Hall

eighteenth- and nineteenth-century French designers, the stringcourse of the Brooks Museum identified a chain of natural historians. Although the names were not arranged chronologically, they too recorded a history and cataloged the individuals crucial to the development of the field.

Several men from the distant community of Rochester, New York, a seat for the natural sciences at the time, played major roles in the creation of a museum at the University. Wealthy Rochester industrialist Lewis Brooks proposed the project and provided most of the funding. This gift marked an important departure: it was the first University building donated by an individual. The unsolicited addition to the grounds, a gesture of post-Civil War reconciliation, was the gift of the Northern philanthropist who never saw the completed building or even visited the campus. John Rochester Thomas, a prominent Rochester architect, was the designer. Another resident of the city, natural historian Henry A. Ward, who was a well-known entrepreneur and broker of scientific specimens and replicas, assembled the collection.

The museum's location corresponded with patterns of growth at the University in the late nineteenth century. Most university buildings, prior to the construction of Fayerweather Gymnasium in the 1890s, hugged the periphery of the Academical Village. Brooks Hall and the University chapel framed the Rotunda Annex prior to its destruction in the 1895 fire. The siting of these buildings indicated the importance of the northern approach to the campus and foreshadowed the outward expansion of the Grounds to the north after 1890.

A building of the Romantic Picturesque era, Brooks Hall was a sophisticated blend of the eclectic styles of the nineteenth century. References to mid-century French design overlay the polychromy and active massing characteristic of the High Victorian Gothic. The steep mansard roof of the central pavilion and the articulation of the wall surface to form central and end pavilions were typical of Second Empire buildings. Ornate and monumental, Second Empire was the style of choice for fashionable public buildings in the United States in the 1860s and 1870s.

While Brooks Hall was an admired addition to the campus in the 1870s, the style fell into disfavor with the advent of the American Renaissance around the turn of the twentieth century. Superintendent of Buildings and Grounds and Jefferson enthusiast William Lambeth despised the building. In an undated speech he grimly predicted its ruin: "When under the shadow of [Jefferson's] spirit any monstrosity appears[,] its abortive and misshapen countenance will invite its own condemnation and will in the end wreak its own destruction. Such was the fate of the Annex, such will be the fate of the Museum." Similarly, US President William Howard Taft, after a visit to the Grounds in the early twentieth century, advised: "Leave it alone. . . . Don't tear it down, don't try to adorn it with columns and porticos. Let it stand untarnished in its perfect majestic ugliness as an everlasting example to succeeding administrations to go their way and sin no more." Interest in the museum's collection waned in the twentieth century as office and classroom space needs rose. The Geological Survey moved in 1908. The museum closed in the 1940s, and the collection was placed in storage and part of it, including the mammoth, destroyed. The battle waged over evolution in Tennessee in 1925 did not envelop the Brooks Museum. Apathy rather than a conservative backlash buried the building's remarkable collection. Seen as incompatible with the Jefferson campus and crowded with unprogrammed functions, Brooks Hall was slated for demolition in the 1970s. A public outcry, led by architectural historians, rescued the building, which now houses the department of anthropology and art classes.

20. University Chapel   *Charles Emmet Cassell, 1884–1890*

The diminutive size of the University chapel gives a quaint, storybook air today to a project that contemporaries saw as anything but fanciful. Jefferson's university had no denominational ties and no building devoted exclusively to worship. The construction of a chapel on the grounds forcefully answered accusations of heathenism, which critics had directed at the University throughout the nineteenth century. Despite the charges of godlessness in Charlottesville, University buildings had housed religious activities from Jefferson's day onward, including a number of locations in the Rotunda. By the end of the nineteenth century, the desire to provide a suitable setting for worship prompted a series of proposals for chapels— each Gothic Revival in style—at various sites on the Grounds.

Like the earlier unbuilt projects, the 1884–90 chapel by Charles Emmet Cassell of Baltimore is styled in the Gothic Revival. Described by the architect as "early pointed," the chapel is an imaginative combination of motifs from a variety of sources. The cruciform plan, steeply sloping roof, use of rough-textured stonework with pointed arched openings, picturesque massing, heavy stepped buttresses, and low square tower are

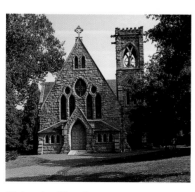

University Chapel

stock motifs drawn from nineteenth-century Gothic parish churches in England and the US. By contrast, elements such as the almond-shaped openings, called mandorla windows, are imaginative and willful departures from the Gothic vocabulary. The gabled portal on the south facade opens into a small narthex lit by stained glass windows. Beyond, in the nave, red granite piers support the heavy wood hammer-beam roof. The individual hammer beams terminate in identical placid grotesques. Brick arches mark the crossing. Stained glass windows light the interior, most believed to have been designed and executed by J. and R. Lamb and Sons. The window in the mandorla of the east transept is by Tiffany Studios. The association of Gothic forms with ecclesiastical architecture in the nineteenth century deepened the contrast with the Jefferson buildings. Although by the latter part of the century the desire to insert a chapel on the Lawn had abated, the new structure was a remarkable departure from the Jefferson tradition—stone rather than brick, Gothic rather than classical, which contemporaries saw as Christian rather than pagan.

With changes in architectural taste to the neoclassical around the turn of the century, enthusiasm for the eccentric chapel dulled. By 1894, John Kevan Peebles, the influential promoter of the return to the Jefferson tradition commented in the *Alumni Bulletin*: "The Chapel is of stone in the Gothic style, and has been the subject of much severe criticism. . . . There can be no doubt that it would have been better to have built it of brick in the classic style." Despite Peebles's and others' criticism, until the 1950s the chapel remained largely unaltered—although not imitated. It is regularly used by student religious groups of a variety of faiths and is a popular place for weddings.

21. Alderman Library and Clemons Library

Alderman Library *Taylor and Fisher, 1936–1938*
Clemons Library *The Architects Collaborative, 1979–1982*

The design and construction of Alderman Library between 1936 and 1938 physically and symbolically reordered the University by removing the presence of the institution's collection of books from the Lawn. Jefferson had placed the Rotunda, which housed the library, at the focal point of his plan for the University, and with it had underscored his faith in the primacy of knowledge. Symbolically brilliant but functionally inadequate as a library, the Rotunda, by the 1930s, could no longer accommodate the rapidly growing numbers of books. The construction of Alderman reunited and centralized the scattered collection at a new location outside of the Academical Village.

Designed by University alumnus R. E. Lee Taylor of Baltimore, Alderman Library followed the spirit of the work that had been executed earlier by the University's Architectural Commission—of which Taylor had been a member. Like his former collaborators, Taylor produced a hybrid Jeffersonian-Georgian mix for a building of a size and scale unknown to Jefferson. To avoid conflict between old and new, Taylor also carefully placed his work apart from the historic campus. At the library, the use of what he called "colonial brick" established a link to the Jefferson campus. The five-part facade diminished the impact of the potentially overpowering mass of the building. The large colonnaded central block was flanked by hyphens, which connected to terminating pavilions. The colonnade of engaged Tuscan half columns of the central core recalled those on the Lawn but blurred Jefferson's careful distinction between the one-story colonnades, which fronted the single-story dormitories, and the colossal orders, used on the pavilions and the Rotunda. To harmonize the new library with the existing campus, Taylor used the steep slope of the site, a dell west of the chapel, to conceal the actual height of the building. The two-story facade on the south fronts a building that is actually five stories on the north.

The new library honored Edwin A. Alderman, the reforming first president of the University, who took office in 1904. A leader of the southern Progressive movement, Alderman set out to recast the University as an instrument of social service. He targeted projects with a social mission, including the development of the medical school and the engineering school as well as the creation of the school of education. In his last address to the University before his death in 1931, Alderman called for the construction of a new library. The completed structure, funded in part by a Public Works Administration grant, was dedicated in 1938 to the University's first president. Charles Keck's 1941 bust of Alderman is inside.

While Alderman Library honored a University giant, it also physically reordered the grounds. The library fixed the northern edge of a large court formed by Monroe Hall, Peabody Hall, Miller Hall, and the north end of the West Range. Jefferson had envisioned expansion of the University in rows of buildings paralleling the Ranges. The Architectural Commission,

Alderman Library, 1936–1938, Taylor and Fisher

McConnell Monument, 1918,
Gutzon Borglum

inspired both by Jefferson and by the contemporary enthusiasm for Beaux-Arts planning principles at other American campuses, proposed a number of buildings and complexes organized around large courts. The Anatomical Theater, a fragment of the Jefferson plan, competed with this succeeding vision. In 1939, the Old Medical Building, which stood near the southeast corner of the new library, became the only Jefferson building on the campus to be demolished. The construction of Alderman Library also necessitated the removal of a relic from the Romantic period, the Gothic Revival gatekeeper's cottage, nicknamed Chateau Front and Back. Built by the University's superintendent of building and grounds, William Pratt, it occupied the steep slope the Architectural Commission had designated for a "large building" in the 1920s. The slope became the Alderman Library site in the 1930s.

Two notable earlier works are nearby. The 1918 James R. McConnell monument is by Gutzon Borglum, best known as the sculptor of the colossal presidential portraits on Mount Rushmore. It stands at the southwest corner of the library and honors a daring University student who had enlisted in the French service and was killed in World War I. Next door, Miller Hall is the oldest surviving non-Jeffersonian academic building on the grounds. Reputedly designed by Professor John W. Mallet, the 1868–1869 one-story brick structure was one of the earliest chemical laboratories in the country. Damaged by an explosion in 1917, it was rebuilt in 1920 as a two-story Colonial revival building in the Jefferson mode, with Eugene Bradbury as the designer. Miller Hall is now slated for demolition to make room for a large addition to Alderman Library to house Special Collections.

While Alderman Library prompted demolition, it also drew later construction nearby. A 1967 addition by J. Russell Bailey, which provided new stack space, covered much of the original north elevation. Another later library to the west designed by Norman Fletcher of The Architects Collaborative of Cambridge honored Harry C. Clemons, the librarian who had overseen the move from the Rotunda to Alderman. Unlike its predecessor, which rose assertively above the edge of a small hollow to bound the northern edge of the court beyond, Clemons Library nestled into the hill, regularizing the grade by means of a series of terraces which stepped down the slope. Plain brick walls, sliced by ribbon windows, marked a decisive departure from the prevailing vocabulary of the campus but aligned with the University's commitment to modernism in the 1960s and 1970s. Crowding its neighbors Alderman Library and Miller Hall, Clemons was assertively modern in its pointed rejection of the University's earlier planning and architectural traditions

22. Peabody Hall and Newcomb Hall

Peabody Hall *Ferguson, Calrow and Taylor, 1912–1914*
Newcomb Hall *Eggers and Higgins, 1952–1958*

Peabody Hall, built between 1912 and 1914 as the home of the new school of education, lay at the heart of President Alderman's reforms. The University's first president secured the funds to create the Curry Memorial School of Education soon after he took office in 1904. The school name honors J. L. M. Curry who, like Alderman, was an eloquent and zealous crusader for public education in the South. A donation from the Peabody Educational Board in 1912 provided the funds for the building. Alderman saw the new education school as an instrument to improve the quality of elementary and secondary education in the state. The building housed the school that trained professional teachers and provided summer in-service training for those already employed in the field. That Alderman moved his personal office and administrative offices to the second floor of the newly finished building indicates his close identity with the mission of the school.

Peabody Hall

An early work of the University Beautiful period, Peabody Hall was sited to defer to the existing complex and dressed in the garb of the familiar. The symmetrical brick building and pedimented Doric portico nodded to Jefferson but looked also to such recent work as Cobb Hall and Minor Hall, which, in turn, ultimately derived from McKim, Mead & White's buildings at the Lawn's south end. The deferential exterior wrapped a thoroughly modern interior. Contemporaries praised the ventilation system, the natural lighting, and such new technologies as the state-of-the-art audiovisual capabilities. Peabody Hall was a model building with a didactic function, ably equipped to house an innovative program. Unfortunately, the much-touted ventilation system worked a little too well. The aroma from the post-Jefferson anatomical laboratory to the west, known as "Stiff Hall," brought frequent complaints from the occupants of Peabody, prior to the demolition of Stiff Hall in the 1950s to make way for Newcomb Hall.

Architects Ferguson, Calrow, and Taylor met with Warren Manning and the University's building committee in 1912 to select the location of Peabody Hall. An entire quadrangle of education buildings appeared on the terrace west of the Academical Village in Manning's 1913 master plan. Although Peabody was intended to be part of the larger complex, the footprint of the building was interestingly absent from the Manning plan. As built, subtle siting knit Peabody Hall to the plan of the Academical Village and other earlier work nearby. Parallel to the West Range, the building is on axis with Hotel C and aligns with the facade of Miller Hall.

Both Peabody Hall and its physical context have changed with time. The later addition of Monroe Hall and Alderman Library formed a quadrangle, although one configured very differently from that planned in 1913. Peabody remained the home of the Curry School prior to the opening of Ruffner Hall in 1973. Today the building contains classrooms and offices.

While Peabody was an instrument of Alderman's educational reform in Virginia, Newcomb Hall, built on the former site of Stiff Hall, was a tool for President Darden's social reworking of the University. The construction of a student activities building was highly controversial in the 1950s. Many fraternity members saw the Student Union as a threatening, anti-elitist challenge to their position at the University. Darden saw the building as a much-needed democratizing agent, which offered social facilities for all students of the University. He secured the funding for the new student union from the General Assembly, and Eggers and Higgins, who designed New Cabell Hall and the McCormick Road dormitories, were retained as architects of the structure, completed in 1958. Newcomb was a late University Beautiful project, and like the McCormick Road dormitories, drew inspiration from the influential restoration of Colonial Williamsburg. Peabody and Newcomb Halls illustrate the subtle shift toward the Georgian Revival during this period. Like Peabody Hall before it, Newcomb was sited to complement the existing context. The large edifice, consisting of a series of offset masses, lined the brow of a steep hill and framed Peabody Hall, which stands to the east. Peabody Hall's portico is the apparent centerpiece of the combined composition, and Newcomb Hall's deferential entries are in the flanking end pavilions. Named in honor of the University's second president, John Lloyd Newcomb, the student activities building, now modified, provides rooms for student dining, services, entertainment, and meetings, as well as offices for administrators and organizations.

23. Monroe Hall   *Architectural Commission, 1929–30; Hartman-Cox, 1984–87*

Monroe Hall, built primarily as a social science building, now houses the McIntire School of Commerce. At many academic institutions in the US, including the University, the rapid growth of the social sciences justified new buildings to house newly separated departments. The University's school of economics and the commerce school numbered among the academic programs housed in Monroe Hall. The undergraduate school of business administration, an offshoot of the school of economics, traces its institutional roots to the study of political economy within Jefferson's school of law. Noted University benefactor Paul McIntire provided funds for the new school of commerce, separate from economics, in 1921; the school bears his name. The building name honors James Monroe whose law offices, now part of Brown College, stood nearby on Monroe Hill.

Like much of the work at the University in the 1920s and 1930s, Monroe Hall is a product of the connection between President Alderman

Monroe Hall

and the Architectural Commission. Alderman promoted the social sciences, and the ascendance of the business school in the early twentieth century was tied to the reforms initiated by the University's first president. Alderman saw the business school, like he viewed other professional programs, as an instrument to train the leaders to guide the development of the New South. The Architectural Commission designed the buildings to house the programs that he promoted. The buildings are an index to Alderman's concerns and created a place for the departments of his pragmatic curriculum.

While the programs and buildings were new, the board carefully knit their work into the existing fabric of the University. To mimic Jefferson's planning, they positioned Monroe Hall to draw the two existing academic buildings nearby into a larger whole. The new structure formed the south edge of a courtyard bordered by Miller and Peabody Halls on the west and by the West Range on the east. Alderman Library, added later on the north, eventually completed the quadrangle. The five-part south facade of Monroe Hall, like that of the later library, diminished the apparent size of the large academic building. The original U-shaped building, executed in brick with classical detailing, was a Georgian-Jefferson mix, typical of the University projects in this period. Subtle siting and careful detailing gently tie Monroe Hall to the Jefferson complex. On the east, the pedimented projecting bay at the south end centers on Hotel E of the West Range. The occupants of Monroe Hall have changed several times. In 1955, the creation of the graduate school of business relocated the commerce and economics schools to the former quarters of the physics department in Rouss Hall. In 1975, when the graduate business school, by then named the Darden School, joined the Law School on the North Grounds, the Commerce School returned home to Monroe Hall. Continued growth of the commerce school hastened expansion.

The sensitive 1984–87 L. G. Balfour addition by Hartman-Cox of Washington, DC, a firm known for sympathetic contextual work, continued the dialogue between Monroe Hall and earlier University buildings. The new wing along the north converted the U-shaped building into a rectangular doughnut, centered on an interior courtyard. In place of the arcade on the north, the five-part elevation of the addition balanced that of Alderman Library across the court. The file of colossal engaged columns, brick corner pilasters, compass head windows, and classical balustrades at the roof were motifs borrowed from the library. Marble tablets bearing quotations were salvaged from the original courtyard of Monroe Hall and are now embedded in the walls of the recessed entrances on the north. The Hume fountain, relocated from the original courtyard to a site west of Monroe Hall, made a place for the new interior courtyard.

24. Brown College and Monroe Hill Dormitories

Brown College *1790s–1994*
Monroe Hill Dormitories *Architectural Commission, 1928–1929*

The history of tiny but centrally located Monroe Hill is a richly layered slice cut from the story of residential life at the University. The historic site of the only building on the grounds that predates the work of the founder also cradles the home of the University's first residential college. Successive additions to the hill mark changes in the size and composition of the student population. Architecturally, the buildings are a series of period pieces, varied interpretations of the work of Jefferson. Socially, the buildings also lay claim to the Jefferson legacy. The aim is the subtle and elusive pursuit of extending education beyond the classroom. The nucleus of the complex is a set of late-eighteenth-century to mid-nineteenth-century buildings. The origins of these structures remain uncertain. Between 1790 and 1799, James Monroe built and occupied the smallest building, which he reputedly used as a law office. The later Greek Revival house is now much altered. The structures were located on the farm later owned by John Perry, which the University subsequently purchased. A portion of the historic Three Notch'd Road ran in the course of the present-day McCormick Road. Clearly, the placement of the buildings—askew from those of the Jefferson complex—responded to the road.

During the nineteenth century, the early buildings housed residential uses. Jefferson considered converting the house to an observatory, and the University proctor used the house as a residence. At mid-century, the complex became a site of institutional reform. In 1846, the Monroe house was turned over to the hotelkeeper for the "State scholars," those students attending the University on scholarships provided by the commonwealth.

Monroe Hill House, 1790s and later. Monroe Hill Range, 1848

In 1848, the University added twelve dormitories adjacent to the house for the same students. The connecting arcades, in the style of the Ranges nearby, tied new to old. As the first student housing constructed outside of the Academical Village, the Monroe Hill dormitories were one of the earliest non-Jeffersonian structures on the Grounds. This project, which provided additional student residences, foreshadowed what would become a perennial problem, the shortage of housing.

By the twentieth century and prior to the construction of Emmet Street, the University golf links extended onto the west slope of Monroe Hill. In 1929, to alleviate the housing shortage, a controversial student housing complex opened on the west slope of Monroe Hill, on a portion of the old golf links. Designed by the Architectural Commission, it overlooked the reworked golf course below. Typical of the Board's work, the buildings presented a Georgian Revival reinterpretation of Jefferson. Pediments, pavilions, and elaborate entries articulate the masses of the large institutional buildings. The composition, the classically detailed entrances, and the arcades also refer to earlier additions to the same site and to Virginia's Georgian heritage. An enclosed quadrangle employed a formal pattern that appeared on numerous American collegiate complexes in the early twentieth century. The cloistered arrangement, which recalled the traditional English system of colleges within a University, was ultimately driven by a nostalgic impulse at a time of growth generally in the American university. The three-story buildings, arranged internally in suites, were modeled on a contemporary student housing project at Harvard. The building names honor University professors. Socially, the multi-story, multi-building compound introduced mass housing to the University, a significant departure from traditional housing options on the grounds—the Lawn, the Ranges, Dawson's Row, the boarding and fraternity houses, and even Randall Hall.

Later developments at the University also affected residential life on Monroe Hill. In 1986, the buildings became the site of the University's first residential college. Originally called Monroe Hill College, it was renamed Brown College in 1994. The early mansion became the principal's house for the new academical village, embedded within the now large and complex university. A sympathetic architectural jewel that makes the complex on the sloping site handicapped accessible is the 1994 elevator by Mitchell, Matthews and Associates. Like the later residential college on Observatory Hill, Brown College was seen as a means to alleviate the personal isolation and anonymity generated by the mushrooming growth of the University. Meals, informal classes, and residential faculty afford opportunities for increased student-faculty interaction outside the classroom. The student residents are selected to assure a diverse population. The goal is to provide a stable environment for the occupants, a rooted subcommunity within the large university, and also an enriching experience of living with peers from a variety of backgrounds.

Clark Hall

25. Clark Hall *Architectural Commission, 1930–1932*

Clark Hall, completed in 1932, became the grand home for the venerable School of Law. The Architectural Commission deemed the location "the most important within the confines of the University," noting that any build-ing placed on it would "be in part view from the lawn." They saw the Law School as a sufficiently prestigious program to recommend that its home cap the small hill southwest of the Central Grounds. While the south end of the Lawn and the land north of the Rotunda had been the focal points of development in the 1890s and early 1900s, during the late 1920s and early 1930s, the Board of Architects identified "the Observatory Road," now McCormick Road, as the logical area for further University growth. They saw the Law Building as the linchpin of the future development of the University in that area. Attorney William Andrews Clark Jr., a member of the Class of 1899, funded the building as a memorial to his wife. A dedication panel in the mural hall records his gift.

Clark Hall, conceived as a grand ornament to the Grounds, was the Architectural Commission's most sophisticated work. While the Board's contemporary projects, such as the nearby Monroe Hill dormitories and Monroe Hall, displayed a reticent Jeffersonian-Georgian blend, Clark Hall is Jefferson in the spirit of Memorial Gymnasium. The pyramidal composition builds in massing toward the center. The five-part facade consists of a large central core flanked by hyphens that terminate in smaller pavilions. The entry at the central portico leads through an entrance lobby to the building's physical and symbolic center: the two-story skylit mural hall. Fluted Ionic three-quarter columns mark the major entrances into the room. The

1930–34 murals, which depict the history of the law, are by Allyn Cox, whose work also appears in the US Capitol. The processional path through the building initially led to an appropriately prominent terminus, the library reading room, on axis at the rear of the building.

Elements of Clark Hall's facade, fragile strands linking building to building across time, tie the Law School to both its former homes. The facade composition of Clark Hall's central block, a recessed hexastyle porch flanked by massive pavilions, echoes that of the Law School's former home in Minor Hall. The interwoven tapestry of the connections includes personal as well as architectural threads. John Kevan Peebles, the architect of Minor Hall, was later a member of the Architectural Commission, the designers of Clark Hall. The inscription in Clark Hall's marble attic by Leslie H. Buckler of the law faculty reads: "That those alone may be servants of the law who labor with learning, courage and devotion to preserve liberty and promote justice." It, too, is a touchstone of the school's collective memory. The inscription, repeated at the entry of the 1990s Law School building on the North Grounds, points back to Clark Hall, one of the school's historic homes on the Central Grounds.

The opening of Clark Hall in 1932 relocated the law department from its overcrowded quarters in Minor Hall. Continued growth after that time has since brought other changes. In 1974, the Law School abandoned its elegant home on the Central Grounds to move to a new facility on the North Grounds. Since the departure of the Law School, the department of environmental sciences has inhabited Clark Hall. Johnson, Craven and Gibson's Kerchof Hall, behind Clark Hall and down the hill, opened in 1956 to house the participants in the Judge Advocate General's School. Prior to the move to the North Grounds, the JAG school shared the academic facilities of the Law School in Clark Hall.

The construction of Clark Hall required demolishing a portion of the legendary student housing complex known as Dawson's Row. In 1835, Martin Dawson had given the University a tract of land to supply it with firewood. His gift was the first donation, other than books, to the new institution. In 1859, the Board of Visitors sold the land and assigned the proceeds to the construction of student housing "on the western part of the University grounds." The gentle arc of brick cottages with bracketed eaves contrasted sharply with Jefferson's neoclassical compound nearby. By the early twentieth century, the earlier dormitories were stylistically jarring and out of step. Classical porticoes, added in 1912, "colonialized" the nineteenth-century complex but did not prevent the demolition of Dawson's Row to make way for new buildings for the growing University—including Clark Hall in the 1930s and Halsey Hall in the 1950s.

26. Garrett Hall, McIntire Amphitheater, and Bryan Hall

Garrett Hall *McKim, Mead & White, 1906–1908*
McIntire Amphitheater *Fiske Kimball, 1920–1921*
Bryan Hall *Michael Graves, 1990–1995*

Garrett Hall

Garrett Hall, which was sited according to the McKim, Mead & White plan for the lateral expansion of the grounds, launched the transformation of the open land south of the West Range. The unfolding development of the area around the McIntire Amphitheater includes a series of comments on Jefferson's work that range in dates from the early to the late twentieth century. McKim, Mead & White also designed Garrett Hall, a two-story red brick building with a hexastyle Tuscan portico. The restrained reinterpretation of the Jeffersonian vocabulary was less grand than the firm's earlier work at the south end of the Lawn. When finished, the building faced a small depression immediately west of Cocke Hall. With the opening of Minor Hall in 1911, the three structures rimmed the upper edges of the tiny dell. The amphitheater, finished in 1921, nestled comfortably into the hollow, deftly regularizing the existing grade. After the completion of the outdoor theater, Garrett Hall stood at the head of the fully bounded complex. Bryan Hall, which opened in 1995, spanned the valley behind the low amphitheater backdrop and, as Cabell Hall had done to the Lawn, screened the enclosed grouping from the landscape beyond.

Garrett Hall has housed a number of functions over time. Built as a refectory, the building brought mass dining—although in elegant surroundings—to the Grounds. The interior of the dignified dining hall was paneled in weathered oak and contained an ornate plaster ceiling—both are still visible. Rejecting the intended intimacy of Jefferson's hotels, the new refectory was large enough to seat almost half the students in a single hall. Used as a Commons until 1958, the building later housed the registrar's and bursar's offices and then the offices of the dean of the College of Arts and Sciences. It was renamed Garrett Hall in 1959 to honor Alexander Garrett, the first bursar of the University.

Like Randall Hall, Garrett Hall followed McKim, Mead & White's master plan. The orderly Beaux-Arts-inspired scheme called for buildings to frame courtyards, which terminated axes leading from the Lawn. The formal plan took no notice of the topography. The building that McKim, Mead,

& White had mirrored across the proposed courtyard in front of Garrett Hall would have sat at the bottom of the steep slope. In 1911, the University's so-called "landscape artist" Warren Manning proposed a more practical use for the site in front of Garrett Hall—an amphitheater. The outdoor theater figured in his City Beautiful-inspired plans in 1908 and 1913. As finally built in 1921, it was repositioned to center on Garrett Hall and tucked into the small hollow bounded by Cocke, Garrett, and Minor Halls. Architect, architectural historian, and head of the new architecture school, Fiske Kimball, was the designer. Noted University benefactor, Paul McIntire, who also endowed the McIntire School of Fine Arts and the McIntire School of Commerce, funded the project. An exemplary neoclassical project, the amphitheater was like Philip Alexander Bruce's contemporary five-volume *History of the University of Virginia, 1819–1919*, commissioned to celebrate the University's centennial. "Greek amphitheaters" were very popular at the time, and contemporaries saw the classically inspired project as in keeping with the Jeffersonian and later architecture of the grounds. Promoters, like Alderman and McIntire, saw the theater as an appropriate setting for anticipated cultural events. City Beautiful ideals, particularly the grand cultural aspirations of the period and the vision of classical forms project out onto the landscape, inspired McIntire Amphitheater.

South of the amphitheater, Michael Grave's Bryan Hall gives the prevailing Jeffersonian classicism at the University a contemporary twist. Named to honor a former rector, John Stewart Bryan, the modest background building defers to the rest of the complex. The structure, which houses the English department, also acts as a link, at the elevation of the buildings that rim it, across the small depression. The dominant element of the restrained facade is a simple elevated colonnade behind the amphiteater backdrop. The milk-bottle-shaped columns are a playful, postmodern caricature of their Jeffersonian predecessors.

Cocke Hall, 1896–1898, left. *McIntire Amphitheater, 1920–1921, Fiske Kimball*, center. *Bryan Hall, 1990–1995, Michael Graves*, right. .

27. Minor Hall and Maury Hall

Minor Hall *John Kevan Peebles, 1908–1911*
Maury Hall *Taylor and Fisher, 1941–1942*

Minor Hall

Minor Hall contained the dignified new home of one of the institution's oldest programs: Law was one of the schools of Jefferson's original University. In the nineteenth century, the University's successive law professors had occupied a number of different quarters on the Lawn, beginning with Pavilion III. By 1900 the law program was overflowing its quarters in the Rotunda basement. Continued calls for a new building repeatedly fell on deaf ears. In 1905, in making the case yet again for construction of a new law building, Dean William Minor Lile noted wryly: "Financially, the Law School is the only fowl in the poultry yard of the University that lays golden eggs. It has always been characteristically modest. It has asked for little, and received less." The Law School was one of the practical and professional programs favored by the University's first president, and Alderman campaigned actively for a new law building. Finally occupied in 1911, Minor Hall was a structure built for a single department. The new law building was named to honor John B. Minor, renowned professor of law, who taught at the University for fifty years, beginning in 1845.

The design history of Minor Hall included a number of notable architects who worked for the University in the early twentieth century. McKim, Mead & White submitted a few sketches but eventually declined the offer to enter the informal competition for the building. The commission went to John Kevan Peebles in 1908. Manning, the University's landscape architect, originally suggested that the law building be placed on the south side of "Long Walk," east of the Rotunda. His proposal touched off a debate. The physicians, who were reluctant to curb the medical school's future expansion, among others, resisted. By November 1908, Manning had relocated the building to a site on axis with Cocke Hall and bordering the small valley that later contained the McIntire Amphitheater.

Minor Hall was an early University Beautiful project, but the difference from Peebles's own Fayerweather Gymnasium, from fifteen years earlier, is striking. While the classicism of the gymnasium was a light appliqué of Jeffersonian references on an essentially Victorian building, Minor Hall is a more integrated and robust exercise, described in *College Topics* in 1909 as

"Colonial . . . to harmonize with the other University buildings." The decisive event separating the two buildings was the work of McKim, Mead & White. Peebles himself acknowledged the debt. In an article published in *Alumni News* in 1910, he noted that Minor Hall was "carefully studied to mass both in height and character with the Commons [now Garrett Hall] and the group at the foot of the Lawn." The large central block, placed between two smaller wings, dominates the rigidly symmetrical facade. The uninflected entry lies behind a columnar screen, which is flanked by massive corner pavilions. The horizontality, serenity, grandeur, and air of calm owed a debt to the contemporary work of the architects of the American Renaissance.

Praised as a "fine edifice" by Philip Alexander Bruce in 1922, Minor Hall was nonetheless soon bursting at the seams. Seriously compromised by state-mandated cuts during construction, the building was obsolete not long after completion. Expansion to the north or west was constrained by the topography: the building had been built into the eastern slope of Monroe Hill. Alumnus William A. Clark Jr. originally planned to finance an addition to Minor Hall. When that proved to be problematic because of the site, he instead agreed to fund the construction of lavish Clark Hall to the west. After the Law School's departure in 1932, Minor Hall served as the home of the Drama department prior to the completion of the Drama Building on Carr's Hill. Today the building contains classrooms and offices, including the Carter G. Woodson Institute for Afro-American and African Studies.

Immediately south of Minor Hall is Maury Hall, built in 1941–42 as the Naval ROTC building near the former site of a portion of Dawson's Row. The building name honors Matthew Fontaine Maury, the noted Virginian known as the "Pathfinder of the Seas." Both the University's naval training program and the building were products of the war effort. Taylor and Fisher, the architects of Alderman Library, designed the structure, which was funded largely by a Work Projects Administration grant. The style of the building echoes the work of the Architectural Commission, of which Taylor had been a member. Maury Hall remains the home of the naval ROTC program.

Halsey Hall, completed in the 1950s as a naval armory, is south of Maury Hall. Taylor and Fisher designed the building, which honors Fleet Admiral William F. Halsey. Built on the site of several of the Dawson's Row cottages, the structure now contains offices and classrooms. South of Bryan Hall is the Luther P. Jackson House. Originally constructed as a parsonage about 1855, the building predated the now-vanished brick pavilions of Dawson's Row. Like the chapel, the parsonage was a fruit of the nineteenth-century debate over the place of religion in the life of the University. The two-story brick building is now the home of the Office of African American Affairs. The buildings in the vicinity, nostalgically called Dawson's Row, were not originally part of the complex whose name they bear.

West Grounds

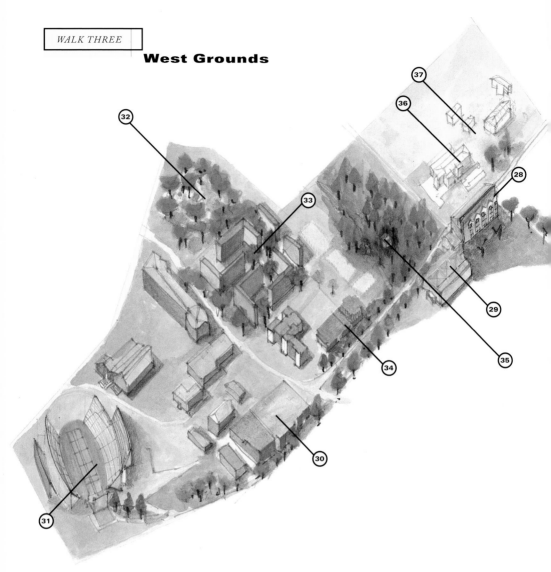

The University Grows
Into the Twentieth Century

Unlike the architecture of the Academical Village and the Central Grounds, the buildings of the West Grounds are threaded along two traffic arteries. McCormick Road, originally known as "the Observatory Road," and Emmet Street cut across the former rural and wooded land west of the historic grounds. In the early nineteenth century, the land west of Monroe Hill contained the now vanished pasture lots for the livestock of the professors and hotelkeepers, the large gardens tended by the hotelkeepers to supply the dining halls, and an orchard. The walk holds an important relic from the University's nineteenth-century life: the shaded cemetery at the foot of Observatory Hill is a tranquil repository of the University's past.

In the early decades of the twentieth century, the gently rolling rural land between Monroe Hill and the cemetery contained the University's rustic golf links. The turn-of-the-century nine-hole course had been lengthened around 1914 and then reconfigured to make room for the Monroe Hill dormitories in 1928. Crimped before, the early golf links disappeared with the construction of the McCormick Road dormitories around 1950.

In 1928, Emmet Street was a two-lane dirt road that ended near Thomson Road. Route 29 was built in 1929 and later widened in 1937. This road marked the western edge of the Central Grounds. McCormick Road, between University Avenue and Alderman Road, follows the path of the old Three Notch'd Road. In the early twentieth century, McCormick Road was lined with residences on the south that overlooked the golf links on the opposite side. The construction of Scott Stadium and Thornton Hall in the early 1930s touched off the radical transformation of the West Grounds.

Two structures for athletics, designed by the Architectural Commission, are the bookends for Walk 3. Memorial Gymnasium is the monumental product of the flamboyant 1920s. Elegantly sited and handsomely planned Scott Stadium is the compromised victim of the Depression that followed within a decade. In between are buildings and landscapes from the University's past and present. Sprigg Lane is a shady retreat, leading to the farmhouse built by one of the University's original faculty members. The eccentric Lambeth House and the ruins of the evocative garden that adjoin it make up a very personal, but now sadly neglected, creation of a prominent member of the University community. To the west, oaks, evergreens, and dogwoods dapple the landscape of the University's burial grounds. To walk through the cemetery is to visit the shades of the University's complex past. Woven in between these earlier works are the dormitories, alumni facilities, and the massive science complex—products of the University's explosive growth in the twentieth century.

28. Memorial Gymnasium   *Architectural Commission, 1921–1924*

Memorial Gymnasium, the most opulent structure on the grounds from the University Beautiful period (1893–c. 1950), climaxed the work that began with McKim, Mead & White's buildings at the south end of the Lawn. The use of red brick and classical ornament forged a link between new and old. However, the gymnasium nodded only faintly to Jefferson and was, in fact, more in keeping with McKim, Mead & White's later projects elsewhere than of their work at the University around the turn of the century. The structure is a single immense volume, whose startling size dwarfed even the Rotunda and which a pair of smaller rectangular blocks flanks. The Architectural Commission designed the exuberant classical building. While the Commission's later work at the University was a relatively demure Georgian-Jeffersonian conflation, the showy center block of the Memorial Gymnasium is its most monumental work.

Memorial Gymnasium was a child of American Renaissance design. The notion that America was the rightful heir of the classical tradition formed the intellectual underpinnings of the American Renaissance and City Beautiful movements. McKim Mead & White's 1906–10 Pennsylvania Station in New York City eloquently embodied the American Renaissance designers' cultural aspirations. "Mem Gym" was a local knockoff of this highly influential work. Like Penn Station, the gymnasium drew loosely on ancient prototypes, such as the Roman Baths of Caracalla and the Baths of Diocletian—particularly suitable models given the function of the University building. The east and west elevations of the large central block are subdivided into a series of bays, each marked by a gabled, parapeted wall dormer containing a semicircular thermal window. Colossal Corinthian orders supporting projecting fragments of entablature flank the bays. The grand classical composition is more nearly reminiscent of imperial Rome than of Jefferson's "specimens" of "chaste" architecture.

Despite the inflated reinterpretation of the Jefferson vocabulary, Memorial Gymnasium defers to the historic campus. The designers placed the imposing building at the bottom of a small hill west of the Lawn to prevent its appearing more prominent than the Rotunda. The height of the gymnasium's engaged, Corinthian orders is deferentially lower than that of the Rotunda. Engaged three-quarter columns line the east elevation of the gym, while pilasters appear on the west—a gentle inflection to mark the importance of the east side, which faces the Lawn and which would have terminated the view as one approached the gymnasium from the Academical Village.

Although Warren Manning had proposed an "advisory board of architects" to oversee the University's design work in 1912, the decision to build Memorial Gymnasium finally prompted the creation of the Architectural Commission. University President Alderman recruited architects Walter Dabney Blair, Fiske Kimball, John Kevan Peebles, and R. E. Lee Taylor to join Superintendent of Buildings and Grounds William Lambeth on

Memorial Gymnasium

the commission formed in 1921. Each of the architects had done or would do work for the University independently. Despite Blair's reservations about the notion of design by committee, the board's collaborative approach dominated University design for a decade: the commission prepared almost all of the University's architecture and planning into the 1930s. Although the four architects collaborated on the design of Memorial Gymnasium, Kimball was identified as the supervising architect of the project. His presence on the Board and subsequent departure may explain why Memorial Gymnasium differs so radically from the Commission's later work.

Although the new gymnasium had originally been planned for a site north of Madison Bowl, the newly formed Architectural Commission suggested a different location in 1921. While the Madison Bowl site would have positioned the new gymnasium conveniently near Madison Hall and Lambeth Field, the relative openness of the Emmet Street site provided room for future expansion. The Commission noted that a building on the alternate site could be developed as a striking ornament to the grounds. With an eye to continued campus growth, it envisioned the gymnasium as the boundary of a quadrangle, which dormitories to the south would complete. Under the spell of the powerful image of the Court of Honor at the 1893 World's Columbian Exposition in Chicago, the Commission reconfigured a small pond on the swampy site to become a great water mirror along the east side of the gym. The "formal lagoon" was drained in 1952.

Like the Monroe Hill dormitories, which were also designed by the Architectural Commission later in the 1920s, Memorial Gymnasium grew out of the dramatic changes to the University in the early decades of the twentieth century. The growth of the student body from 706 in 1905 to 1,270 in 1920 rendered the modestly sized Fayerweather Gymnasium obsolete by the 1910s. Reform-minded University President Alderman linked physical conditioning to intellectual health when he made the case for the larger gym to accommodate the growing student population in 1915. To solicit student funding for the project, he suggested dedicating the proposed facility as a memorial to the sixty-six University students killed in World War I.

The opening of Memorial Gymnasium in 1924 relocated the University's athletic facilities to a grand new facility. The structure remained the seat of the University's basketball contests until the opening of University Hall in 1965. Since the departure of most of the intercollegiate athletic program, the facility has housed intramural sports and other recreational activities.

29. Central Grounds Parking and University of Virginia Bookstore

Walker Parking Consultants with Mariani and Associates, 1989–1994

Central Grounds Parking and UVA Bookstore

The Central Grounds Visitor Parking deck is the most recent monument to the automobile at the University. The completion of the four-story facility on the site of a former surface parking lot resolved the pressing need for parking located conveniently near the Central Grounds. Built into the towering bank below Newcomb Hall, the structure not only provides access up the steep slope but also makes use of a difficult site. The University Bookstore, relocated from nearby Newcomb Hall, crowns the structure.

Despite the usefulness of the parking deck, it is an assertive rather than retiring newcomer. At the new structure, processing, circulation, and efficiency collide with hierarchy, decorum, and propriety. In Jefferson's original scheme, the most important building, the library, occupied the most important position at the focal point of the complex. Through the manipulation of size, shape, position, and detailing, Jefferson identified the Rotunda as the centerpiece, the heart and soul, of the Academical Village. The rational and ordered arrangement of forms provided a clear diagram of the institutional hierarchy: clarity was a hallmark of Jefferson's architecture. In the design of the parking garage, drive-by legibility and ease of access replaced architectural clarity and institutional identity, and circulation triumphed over the embodiment of ideals. The admirable goals of orienting visitors to the grounds and of minimizing the friction from touring on unfamiliar turf produced the questionable decision to make a parking deck a focal point of the campus. The building's color palette, massing, and detailing are an attempt to harmonize with and also to stand out from the lively and flamboyant, yet academically correct, Memorial Gymnasium next door.

Thornton Hall

30. Thornton Hall *Architectural Commission, 1930–1935*

With the construction of Thornton Hall, the University placed the first academic building west of the Emmet Street edge and initiated the transformation of the former agricultural, and later residential, land along McCormick
Road. The sites originally considered for the new engineering school were
near Clark Hall and closer to the traditional academic core. These proposed
locations were subsequently abandoned, since they would have required
either the demolition of a portion of historic Dawson's Row or the expense
of placing a large building on a steep grade. The architects selected instead
the fairly level site further out along "the Observatory Road," now known as
McCormick Road.

Thornton Hall, designed by the Architectural Commission, capped
the career of this University institution. The gentle interweaving of
Georgian and Jeffersonian motifs is a familiar theme in their work during
the University Beautiful period. While the hipped roofs, belt courses, and
compass-head windows are standard Georgian Revival fare, the liberal use
of arcades establishes a link to Jefferson. Atypically, though, the designers
drew on the sturdy, straightforward formal vocabulary of the Ranges, red
brick and arcades rather than columns and embellished entrances, to create a compound for the growing engineering school. To diminish the visual
impact of the large mass of the building, the designers also looked to the
work of the founder: they subdivided the large building into smaller units
organized around a central court. John Kevan Peebles, the chairman of the
Architectural Commission, died in 1934, prior to the completion of the
building. Thornton Hall was the commission's final project.

The building honored William Thornton, first dean of the engineering school. The reference to the Jefferson idiom in a building honoring the
prominent engineering educator was particularly appropriate, since

Thornton, like Peebles, had argued for the return to the Jefferson vocabulary for the University's architecture at the turn of the twentieth century. Like other projects of the period, such as Alderman Library and the Bayly Art Museum, Thornton Hall was funded by a New Deal Public Works Administration grant. While additional buildings now house portions of the school of engineering, Thornton Hall remains their central home.

Although Thornton Hall was new in the 1930s, the instruction in engineering at the University had a lengthy history. Courses in civil engineering were offered intermittently beginning in 1835. Prior to 1895, the Rotunda Annex housed engineering classes. The Rotunda fire left the engineers without a physical home. While the new Mechanical Laboratory, now known as Cocke Hall, housed the young department in 1897, it soon outgrew these facilities. The growth of the engineering school in the early twentieth century arose from the reforms initiated by President Alderman. As one component of his campaign to provide graduates trained to guide the development of the New South, Alderman promoted the training of the engineers and, at the University, he campaigned for better quarters for the engineering program. Thornton Hall, completed after Alderman's death, grew from both his interest and the heightened prominence of engineering in the early twentieth century.

Although Thornton Hall was not originally intended to spawn adjacent buildings housing similar academic disciplines, it was the initial seed that subsequently flowered later in the century as the extensive science and engineering complex. While the building's placement on "the Observatory Road" in the 1930s had been guided by utility rather than by future planning considerations, by the 1950s, University administrators were actively promoting the area around the engineering school as a science center. With the completion of the Physics Building in 1954, Gilmer Hall in 1963, and the Chemistry Building in 1969, the complex grew steadily. The 1965 University Development Plan only codified a zoning of the area that had already developed loosely over time.

Functionally, the science buildings, like Thornton Hall, served as envelopes for modern research activities. The designers of these later projects, like the Board of Architects before them, gestured, although progressively more faintly, to the Founder's work. The architects of the Chemistry Building, Anderson, Beckwith and Haible with Stainback and Scribner, abstracted the forms of the Jefferson vocabulary for use on a building housing a modern function. In a 1965 *Alumni News* article on the design of the new structure, the author noted: "The facade [of the Chemistry

Gilmer Hall addition, 1984–1987, R. M. Kliment and Frances Halsband

Building] facing Gilmer Hall across an open court, will contain vertical white elements that suggest Mr. Jefferson's architecture for the original academical village. It is thus considered an architectural 'bridge' between the unchanged old University and the new science and engineering complex that is growing up near Scott Stadium." With time, the connection to the Jefferson tradition grew even more tenuous. VVKR's 1985 Materials Science and Engineering Building's unarticulated brick walls, ribbon windows, and flat roof were aggressively modern. The planar white wall slabs that sheathe part of the structure referenced the vocabulary of the International Style, not the local style. Despite the "bridges" and the intentions of 1965, with projects such as the Materials Science and Engineering Building, the gulf between old and new widened.

31. Scott Stadium and Aquatic and Fitness Center

Scott Stadium *Architectural Commission, 1929–1931*
Aquatic and Fitness Center *The Hughes Group with Michael Dennis, 1993–1996*

Scott Stadium, 1929–1931, Architectural Commission

Scott Stadium, the first University-built structure west of Emmet Street, other than the Observatory complex, was, like Memorial Gymnasium, a product of the sustained enthusiasm for athletics as spectacle in the 1920s. While Lambeth Field had been hailed as beautiful and grand in the 1910s, by the 1920s its seating capacity could no longer accommodate the growing number of student and alumni spectators. Alumnus and rector Frederic W. Scott funded the new oval, two-part stadium, which seated 25,000. The University's Architectural Commission, led by John Kevan Peebles, designed and built the facility between 1929 and 1931.

The fragmentation of the University's athletic facilities began with the siting of Scott Stadium. With its placement, the Architectural Commission abandoned its own early-1920s plans for an athletic compound centered around Memorial Gymnasium and Lambeth Field. The designers examined four locations before choosing the site of the large arena. Economic and site-access issues, rather than the establishment of campus zoning priorities, guided their selection. The Scott Stadium site was attractive for several reasons. The topographic configuration of the land suited the grading required for a large athletic arena. The projected traffic could be handled most efficiently at that location, and the University already owned the large tract of land.

Aquatic and Fitness Center, 1993–1996, The Hughes Group with Michael Dennis

The architects' concerns also included aesthetics. They cited the scale of the new projects under design, radically different from those of the Jefferson campus, as a reason for placing the new construction away from the Academical Village. Spatial separation disguised a disjunction. Jefferson's work at the University established the point of departure for the work of the Architectural Commission. Nonetheless, by the early twentieth century, the Jefferson model, in both scale and mass, was no longer adequate for the new projects that were being designed. The commission had as its stated goal to harmonize its new design works with that of the existing campus. In reality, the commission saw the old and new work as incompatible. Its solution was to treat the Jefferson campus as a relic, preserved through isolation.

Like other works of the Architectural Commission during the University Beautiful period of the early 1900s, the architectural vocabulary of Scott Stadium sought to draw a connection to the by-then isolated Jeffersonian campus. Scott's goal was to create the "most beautiful stadium in America." The architects and patron concurred that the arcaded brick exterior walls and the curving colonnaded walkway and pavilions around the perimeter at the top of the seating, reminiscent of those in the Lambeth Colonnade, were elegant solutions that would forge a link to the historic campus beyond. While cost dictated a reconsideration, and eventual elimination, of much of the proposed grand classical detailing, the use of brick survived the economizing cuts.

The later addition of upper decks has obscured the simplicity of the original execution. An artificial turf field, installed in 1974, has now come and gone. A new sod field initiated the 1995 season. Currently, new upper-deck seating at the south end is planned. Later additions to the University's athletic facilities in the orbit of Scott Stadium include the Aquatic and

Fitness Center. The mildly postmodern structure is in the spirit of the Gilmer Addition nearby on McCormick Road. Less Jeffersonian than Stern's addition to the Observatory Hill Dining Hall across Alderman Road, the brick and glass Aquatic and Fitness Center opened in 1996. Michael Dennis, the design consultant for The Hughes Group, was the architect.

32. University Cemetery   *1828–present*

The cemetery, situated on a knoll at the foot of Observatory Mountain, is the oldest memorial landscape at the University. Jefferson's Academical Village enshrined aesthetic and civic values but ignored individual achievement and collective memory. He left it to his successors to develop the fabric of institutional memory and to inscribe that record on the landscape. Sculpture now dots the grounds—images commissioned by the heirs to honor their heroes—and building names catalog individual contributions and form a roll call of University worthies.

The cemetery preserves a selective history, a slice cut through the contours of the University's past. The burial grounds were set aside soon after his death on the land west of the Academical Village and enclosed by 1829. The first individual buried at the site was Dr. Henry William Tucker, brother of a University faculty member, George Tucker. Henry William Tucker died of typhoid fever in 1828. His grave lies along the west wall of the old cemetery. That same year John Temple was the first student to be interred in the new cemetery. His grave is to the north of the Tucker plot. Temple died of typhoid fever. Temple's burial at the University, away from his home in King and Queen County, Virginia, was common in a period in which it was often not possible to take bodies home for interment. The frequent epidemics that plagued the University in the nineteenth century left a mark not only in the establishment of the University Cemetery but also in the construction at mid-century of the infirmary at the south end of the East Range.

Tombstones honoring prominent figures from the University's unfolding history dot the site. Charles Bonnycastle, a member of the original faculty, was the first University professor buried in the cemetery. A simple marker identifies the grave of Edwin Alderman, first president of the University. Buried in the eastern part of the cemetery are William Mynn Thornton, the first dean of the engineering school, whose home in Thornton Hall bears his name; John B. Minor, eminent professor of law, for

University Cemetery, 1828–present

whom Minor Hall was named; Philip Alexander Bruce, author of the centennial history of the University; and John Lloyd Newcomb, second president of the University. The western section holds the graves of Jesse W. Beams, a prominent professor of physics; Harry Clemons, the University librarian commemorated by Clemons Library; Frederick Doveton Nichols, professor of architecture who was instrumental in the 1976 restoration of the Rotunda; and Edgar F. Shannon Jr., fourth president of the University.

The fabric of the cemetery also quietly documents significant moments in the University's past. John A. G. Davis, whose murder by a student in 1840 prompted the creation of the University's well-known honor code, is buried in the precinct. During the Civil War, the University housed a hospital and over a thousand soldiers are buried—most in unmarked graves—in the Confederate section of the cemetery. Caspar Buberl's 1893 monument at the center honors the fallen and feeds the memory of the Lost Cause. The inscription on the base asserts: "Fate denied them victory but crowned them with glorious immortality."

The nineteenth-century campaign to remove burials from crowded churchyards to rural parks, known as the rural cemetery movement, only obliquely touched the cemetery on the grounds. Since the University was already isolated from the city and not affiliated with a church, the overt rejection of urban and ecclesiastical settings that fueled the establishment of rural cemeteries elsewhere did not dictate the placement of this cemetery. In contrast to the picturesque planning characteristic of the pioneering nineteenth-century projects, like Mt. Auburn Cemetery in Cambridge, Massachusetts, the placement of monuments in rows at the University burial grounds follows a traditional arrangement. Nonetheless, both the shady park-like setting of the cemetery today and the isolation from the Academical Village are in line with progressive nineteenth-century notions about interment.

Naturally, the growth of the University community over time has placed demands on the size of the compound. Although additions to the cemetery were approved in 1883, 1914, and 1938, no future expansions are planned. On the north, the new columbium wall, completed in 1992, contains vault space for funerary urns. With this addition, the cemetery again functions as part of a living organism, changing with time as a memorial landscape honoring the members of the University community.

33. McCormick Road Residences *Eggers and Higgins, 1946–1951*

The McCormick Road residences were only one of a number of facilities built to accommodate the rapidly growing and changing student population in the post-World War II period. The temporary Copeley Hill housing, located on the site that now contains University Hall, provided residences for a new type of student, the returning veterans, who were accompanied by their families. Nearby, Mary Munford Hall was a dormitory for women, built at a time when ladies were primarily admitted only to the graduate and professional programs. The ten-building McCormick Road dormitories housed first-year men, members of the University's growing, but still primarily male, student body. The new student union in Newcomb Hall contained facilities for a variety of activities open to all students, offering an alternative to the exclusive

McCormick Road Residences, 1946–1951, Eggers and Higgins

social life traditionally dominated by the fraternities. With the exception of the Copeley Hill housing, these projects were part of the unprecedented expansion and conversion of the grounds during the Darden presidency. Today the McCormick Road dormitories house first-year students, male and female.

Apart from the demographic changes, the construction of the new dormitories contributed to the gradual transformation of the landscape along McCormick Road from rural and residential to institutional. The University's Architectural Commission had identified the land along "the Observatory Road" as the area for University growth in the 1930s. Gradually, the housing to the south of McCormick Road disappeared to make way for the University's growing science complex. The site of the dormitories had been part of the University's turn-of-the-century golf links. The large man-made terrace that formed the platform for the housing complex obliterated the gently rolling hills of the former golf course.

The McCormick Road dormitories are a late project of the University Beautiful period in the first half of the 1900s. Reminiscent of the Monroe Hill dormitories of 1928–1929, an earlier work from the same period that had been motivated by similar concerns, the McCormick Road Dormitories were a vast housing project, organized and clad in the garb of the familiar. The architects Eggers and Higgins were also the designers of New Cabell Hall and of Newcomb Hall. Like Newcomb Hall, the Georgian Revival dormitories were in debt not only to the traditional architecture of the Grounds but also to the influential restoration of Colonial Williamsburg. A series of pavilions, linked by tiered dormitory rooms, articulated the edges of the long central court. The treatment is a recasting of Jefferson's formula for the Lawn. The buildings of the complex are arranged to frame large outdoor rooms—an allusion to both the Founder's and to the Architectural Commission's earlier work.

The complex builds other bridges to the past. Each of the ten buildings honors a noted University professor: Charles Bonnycastle and John

Patten Emmet from the original faculty and the others from more recent times. Planting also reinforced the connection between new and old. Alden Hopkins, the landscape architect for the contemporary "restoration" of the gardens in the Academical Village, offered advice on the addition of trees to alleviate the harshness and bareness generated by the growth and sweeping, large-scale construction during the period that President Darden described as the "red mud era." The 1984–87 later addition to Gilmer Hall across the street cleverly completes the composition set up in the main court of the earlier student housing complex. A bold semicircular element with a Palladian window now terminates the strong axis framed by the Eggers and Higgins dormitories. R. M. Kliment and Frances Halsband's postmodern addition recalls the relationship between the Rotunda and the other buildings on the Lawn.

34. Ruffner Hall

Caudill Rowlett Scott with Rawlings, Wilson and Fraher, 1970–1973

Ruffner Hall, 1970–1973, Caudill Rowlett Scott with Rawlings, Wilson and Fraher

Ruffner Hall, the current seat of the Curry School of Education, is a product of the dramatic growth of the University in the twentieth century. The changes rendered the school's historic home in Peabody Hall obsolete. Between 1914, the year of the completion of Peabody Hall, and 1970, when the education school prepared to move into its new facility, the University's enrollment increased tenfold. By the time of the move to Ruffner Hall, the education school was scattered across the grounds, with portions operating out of six different buildings. The move reunited the school under a common roof.

Like the education school itself, the site of Ruffner Hall also changed greatly in the intervening years following the construction of Peabody Hall. Situated on a portion of the old golf links, the building faces Emmet Street, a road that had been built in the late 1920s. The bridge that ties Ruffner Hall to Monroe Hill today testifies to the increasingly heavy auto traffic on the artery that separates the Central Grounds and the West Grounds. Completed in 1973, Ruffner Hall displays design concerns of the University's Campus Suburban era after mid-century. Like much of the University architecture constructed during the period, the style is a modern abstract composition of prismatic volumes with sharply cut openings. The facade composition is assertively asymmetrical. Instead of a traditional treatment—an embellished portal at the center of the façade—the entry is downplayed and pointedly not centered. In fact, the location of the main entry is ambiguous. The architects, Caudill Rowlett Scott, executed a number of academic buildings around the same time that were organized around the circulation armature. Ruffner Hall, too, is threaded on a circulation spine. The extension of the pedestrian bridge that crosses Emmet Street is a contrasting horizontal element in concrete, woven into and around the planar brick masses of the building. Unlike the earlier buildings on the Central Grounds, the placement of Ruffner Hall responds to the road rather than to other buildings. The planning of grand courtyards, so important in the 1930s, is gone. Parking, an increasingly important design constraint, dominates the building's foreground.

Nonetheless, even here, there are echoes of the past. Despite the Modern architectural vocabulary, the red brick and off-white trim—here, heavily textured concrete—gesture to the dominant local vocabulary. The colonnade of brick piers is a contemporary restatement of Jefferson. Using words that echo the earlier descriptions of Peabody Hall, contemporaries praised the building as an innovative structure supporting a dynamic program. Names serve a commemorative function. The McGuffey Reading Center, established in 1946, honors the University's noted mid-nineteenth-century professor of moral philosophy, William Holmes McGuffey, whose numerous editions of the influential *Eclectic Reader* made him "America's schoolmaster." The department named for J. L. M. Curry, the late-nineteenth-century pioneering reformer of Southern education inhabits a building named for William H. Ruffner, the father of the modern public school system in Virginia. Just as the Emmet Street bridge creates a physical link to the old grounds, these names, too, tie the school to its historic roots at the University.

35. Lambeth House *c. 1912* and Gardens *c. 1916*

The residence at 1912 Thomson Road was the home of a University legend, Dr. William A. Lambeth. The academic and professional accomplishments of the reputedly onetime circus performer turned Renaissance man are almost mythical. Born in 1867 in Thomasville, North Carolina, Lambeth held both a MD and a PhD in geology from the University of Virginia. He also studied at the Harvard University School of Physical Training. At the University, Lambeth served as a professor of hygiene, of physical education, and a director of athletics. For his tireless work in the area of amateur sports, he is often referred to as the father of intercollegiate athletics at the University of Virginia. Lambeth Field honors these contributions. As superintendent of buildings and grounds from 1905 to 1928, he oversaw the vast expansion of the grounds under President Alderman and worked with Warren Manning on the first comprehensive master plan for the University. Steeped in the Jeffersonian tradition, he co-authored with Manning *Thomas*

Lambeth House and Gardens

Jefferson as an Architect and a Designer of Landscapes, an early study of Jefferson's design work. An ardent Italiophile, he toured regularly in that country and was instrumental in the creation of the Italian studies program at the University. Decorated by the Italian government for his work in promoting understanding between that country and the United States, he also furnished the Italian Room in the Romance Pavilion on the East Lawn.

Lambeth's house reflects the owner's varied interests. Around 1912, he began construction on Villino Lambeth, set in the rural lands west of the grounds. The house to the north, which became Alumni Hall, had not yet been started. Morea stood nearby. To the south ranged the University golf links. After completing their villa, the Lambeths nonetheless remained in the athletic director's residence next to Fayerweather Gymnasium until the construction of the Bayly Museum on Rugby Road necessitated the demolition of that house in 1933. The Lambeth house on Thomson Road gave the dominant local idiom an Italian twist. The central block of the brick house contains a Jeffersonian full Doric portico but is topped with an eccentric red pantile roof, similar to that used on the contemporary Lambeth Colonnades nearby. Set on a hill, it overlooked the formal gardens, Meadow Creek, and the Dell below.

The formal gardens, begun around 1916, were modeled on the Italian gardens that Lambeth admired. Twin casinos, now in ruins, served as teahouses and flanked a garden pergola, which overlooked a pair of rectangular pools and a circular flowerbed, on axis with the gates. From the pergola there were distant views of the pale blue mountains to the west. To the east, prior to the construction of Memorial Gymnasium, there were views of the lake, which had covered the site, and of the University beyond. Sculpture, an index to Lambeth's heroes and interests, included a copy of the *Dying Gaul*, a bust of Alderman, and a capital from the old Rotunda. The extant brick gate was the entrance from the east. The 1991 fighting stags, by University alumnus W. H. Turner, are a recent addition to the site.

Subsequent events have transformed the rural villa. Lambeth died in 1944. He left the house and gardens to the University that was the center of his life's work. His wife remained in the house until 1963. The Curry School of Education currently uses the building. The construction of Route 29 in the 1920s and a later widening of the road in the 1930s dammed Meadow Creek, causing periodic flooding of a portion of the gardens. The development of the former golf links, beginning in the late 1940s with the construction of the McCormick Road dormitories, contributed to the problem. Today, the evocative ruins present a poignant reminder of a legendary figure from the University's past.

36. Alumni Hall

c. 1915; Edmund S. Campbell, Willard Edward Stainback and Louie L. Scribner, 1949–1950;
Johnson, Craven and Gibson, 1981–1983

Alumni Hall

The Alumni Association began in 1838 as the Society of Alumni. Renamed the General Alumni Association in 1902, the organization's goals and objectives remain the same: providing services to the alumni and the University community, fundraising, promoting fraternity among graduates, and maintaining alumni records. As part of its mission to promote ties between the University and its former students, the alumni association collaborated on the publication of periodicals, such as the *Alumni Bulletin*, beginning in 1894, and the *Alumni News*, beginning in 1913. Alumni dues support the organization.

Alumni Hall is the seat of the Alumni Association. Seeking permanent quarters in the early twentieth century, the organization, in 1903, agreed to pool its resources with those of the promoters of the athletic field house to construct a shared building. By 1910, this plan had been abandoned. Meanwhile, the peripatetic association occupied offices in several locations, including Hotel D on the East Range and the Corner Building. In 1936, the Alumni Association purchased, renovated, and moved into its current home, conveniently located on Emmet Street opposite the indoor athletic arena, Memorial Gymnasium. The building, originally constructed as a private residence and then later used as a fraternity house, was a two-story rectangular frame structure with a colossal Tuscan portico. The pedimented portico with a tympanum lunette window was a familiar motif drawn from the ubiquitous Jeffersonian idiom.

The rapid growth of the University, due in part to the influx of veterans after World War II, strained facilities all over the grounds, including those of Alumni Hall. In 1947, the managers of the University Development Fund targeted a number of needed building projects, including an addition to Alumni Hall. The addition to the Alumni Hall was funded as a memorial to the alumni who had died in the war. Campbell, the head of the University's architecture program, collaborated with Stainback and Scribner, both early graduates of the University's architecture program, on the expansion, completed in 1950. Campbell had planned and overseen the 1936 remodeling of Alumni Hall and had been a member of the Architectural Commission in the 1920s and 1930s. The extensive later addition to Alumni Hall was under construction when he died suddenly in 1950. The architects reused the formerly frame building of Alumni Hall as the central block of a brick structure flanked by hyphens and terminal wings. As a project designed late in University Beautiful period (1893–c. 1950) on the threshold of the Suburban Campus period (c. 1950–c. 1976), the central core, the oldest part of the structure, is pure Colonial Revival in the Jeffersonian mode. On the flanking wings, the parapeted gable ends and the unarticulated, crisply cut arched openings make a tentatively modern interpretation of the bay motif of Memorial Gymnasium. The allusion to the athletic arena across the street forges a link between the alumni activities housed within and the athletic programs around which they are often organized. The University's third President Colgate Darden and his wife gave the 1955 brick wall enclosing the side garden as a tribute to J. Malcolm Luck, the long-serving director of alumni affairs.

Continued growth necessitated another expansion. Johnson, Craven and Gibson, also the architects of the Alderman Road residences, designed a large addition, completed in 1983, which provided new office space on the north and an assortment of entertainment and gathering spaces on the west. While Campbell's wings made a minimalist restatement of a familiar motif, the later addition by Johnson, Craven and Gibson, well known for their Colonial Revival work, draws directly on Jefferson. The north wing, visible on the facade is finished with a pedimented gable end containing a lunette window. A more recent interior remodeling, completed in 1998, created a long gallery that houses a permanent exhibit about the University during the late-nineteenth- and twentieth centuries. Sculptor's Donald De Lue's 1975 bronze of Jefferson, presented as a confident and assertive man, also stands inside.

37. Sprigg Lane *1834–1984*

The blows of a number of explosive University issues have touched quiet and shady Sprigg Lane. Although the timeless and sleepy street appears to

Sprigg Lane Residences, 1982–1984, Robert A. M. Stern with Marcellus, Wright, Cox and Smith

be a restful fragment from a simpler time, its development has frequently pitted the old University against the new, preservation against progress, and memory against maximization. Sprigg Lane was not originally developed by the institution that now owns much of it. Nonetheless, the architecture and landscapes along the street chronicle many of the changes to the University in the nineteenth and twentieth centuries. At 209 Sprigg Lane,

Morea House, 1834–1835, attributed to John Patten Emmet

Morea, built within a decade of Jefferson's death, stands as a rare survivor of the numerous houses built near the grounds in the early and mid-nineteenth century. Across the street, at 210 Sprigg, the Bemiss House is a University Beautiful era project that is the domestic analogue of contemporary institutional projects at the University, such as nearby Memorial Gymnasium. The 1930s Jeffersonian Revival house is soaked in the predominant local idiom. Mary Munford Hall, from the 1950s, was a product of the storm of controversy over the admission of women to the University. Next door, the 1980s Sprigg Lane residences illustrate the polarization beneath the surface of the University's neotraditional design period. The divisive issue here was neither the style, which was deferential and demure, nor the function, which was by then no longer gendered or politicized, but, instead, the siting, on a portion of the historic Morea tract. The sequence of the buildings and later changes to them charts the changing priorities at the University in the nineteenth and twentieth centuries.

Long before the construction of Sprigg Lane and of the nearby street that bears his name, John Patten Emmet, one of the original faculty members, built Morea as his home in the shadow of the University. Emmet was the first professor of natural history, appointed in 1825, and was responsible for instruction in areas including chemistry, botany, and comparative anatomy. Emmet gave up his home in Pavilion I in the Academical Village for the farmhouse he built on land just outside the Grounds in

Bemiss House, 1930s, Marshall Swain Wells

1834–35. While Emmet had only reluctantly supported the creation of the botanical gardens, a project proposed by Jefferson but never built, he was a tireless horticultural experimenter on his own farm. He planted Chinese mulberries to investigate the nurture of silkworms. The name Morea is taken from the Latin *morus*, the word for mulberry tree. He also cultivated wine for grapes and brandy and planted cuttings from the horticultural spoils taken from the Lewis and Clark expedition. The osage orange tree on the grounds was one of their discoveries.

The farmhouse itself has been expanded several times. After Emmet's early death in 1842, his wife took in boarders—a familiar pattern at the dormitory-poor University in the nineteenth century. The original house is the two-story central block. Jefferson's influence is felt in the much later pedimented central entry as well as in the apparently early Tuscan columns and Chippendale rail at the second floor porch. Later additions adapted the dwelling to the needs of the occupants, including a series of University professors who inhabited Morea into the twentieth century. Sprigg Lane bears the name of one of these later inhabitants. The remaining three acres of the Emmet farm, which also contained the farmhouse, were donated to the University in 1960 and became a guesthouse for visiting dignitaries. The Albemarle Garden Club undertook the project of replanting the historic grounds in 1963. Labels identify the specimen plants on the site.

The Bemiss House, built across the street in the 1930s, is roughly contemporary with Fiske Kimball's reverential homage to Jefferson, Shack Mountain, in Albemarle County. The designer of the Bemiss House was one of Kimball's students, Marshall Swain Wells. The symmetrical brick house, with a pedimented Doric portico and tympanum lunette, draws on the memory of the early-nineteenth-century regional architecture in the Jefferson mold. Like the contemporary institutional work of the Architectural Commission, the Bemiss House drank deeply from the roots of this local tradition. While the commission's work adapted the Jeffersonian vocabulary to the design of large institutional buildings, domestic buildings, like the Bemiss House, were of a scale similar to that of Jefferson's work and, therefore, were more literal in their imitation. With a 1990s addition, the former residence now houses the University Press of Virginia.

Mary Munford Hall and Gwathmey House are products of the charged controversy in the twentieth century over the admission of women to Jefferson's predominantly male university. Although there had been earlier exceptions, women were not freely admitted to the graduate and professional schools until 1920 and as undergraduates until 1970. The Mary Munford dormitory, which opened in 1952, was not the first women's dormitory on the grounds, but it was an early facility built specifically for women. The stylistic formula was by this time entirely familiar: a light appliqué of Jeffersonian details on a Georgian Revival frame. The names honor a long-serving Board of Visitors member Mary Cooke Branch Munford, who had campaigned actively for the admission of women since the 1910s. Gwathmey House, an addition to Munford Hall completed in 1970, honors Roberta Hollingsworth Gwathmey, dean of women from 1935–67. The neo-Georgian building harmonizes with its neighbor but contrasts sharply with the modern vocabulary of the earlier Alderman Road residences. The second dormitory opened as women were freely admitted to the University for the first time. These two buildings now house mostly upper-class students. The construction of yet another set of dormitories next door set off a new controversy—this time over land use rather than ladies. In the 1980s, the University proposed the construction of the new Sprigg Lane Residences on the Morea site. The two-building complex was sited to defer to the Morea gardens. The tentative and wan Georgian Revival buildings, which harmonize with the student housing next door, were designed by Robert A. M. Stern, a leading light of the Jeffersonian Revival at the University in the 1980s and 1990s, with Marcellus Wright, Cox, and Smith as the local associates. What appear to be Georgian chimneys are actually ventilation elements. The insertion of these latest dormitories in the 1980s brought to the fore questions about the appropriate style for the architecture of the University, as well as debate about land use and competing precedents and histories, as the growing University attempted to use its past in laying a path to the future.

Health Sciences Center

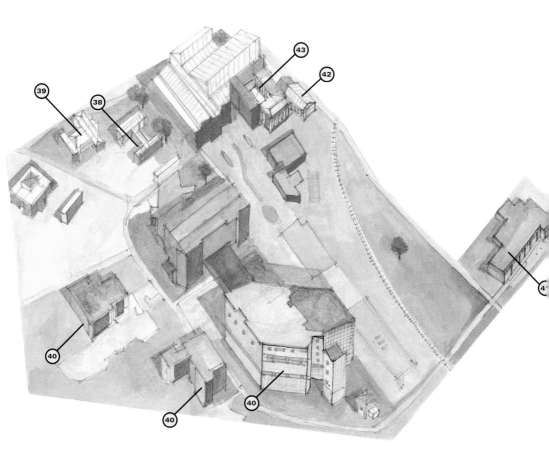

38	**Old University Hospital and McKim Hall**
39	**Cobb Hall**
40	**McLeod Hall, Jordan Hall, Health Sciences Library, and University Hospital**
41	**Stacey Hall**
42	**Corner Building**
43	**Medical School Building**

Medical Education Thrives
Beyond the Academical Village

The Health Sciences Center contains the University's medical service and medical education buildings. The University's first medical building, apart from Pavilion X, was Jefferson's Anatomical Theater, west of the Academcial Village. The construction of the infirmary in the 1850s and particularly of the original Hospital around the turn of the century, established a firm toehold for the Medical School on the area to the east of the Academical Village. The vast health sciences complex includes the no-longer-visible old Hospital buildings, the old Medical School Building, McKim Hall, and Cobb Hall near the Central Grounds, as well as their later-twentieth-century counterparts and replacements across Jefferson Park Avenue.

Medical education at the University, and the buildings that supported it, developed slowly during the nineteenth century. Jefferson's original curriculum included a school of anatomy but no hospital. The sparsely populated setting for the University did not justify such a building. Robley Dunglison, a member of the original faculty, was the lone professor of medicine and surgery, although John Emmet, the professor of natural history, also provided instruction in medical subjects. For much of the nineteenth century, the school's emphasis was on theory instead of on professional education: medicine was presented as one component of a general liberal education rather than as preparation for professional practice. Jefferson's Anatomical Theater provided students the opportunity to observe rather than to participate in laboratory work. Graduates of the University's medical school went elsewhere, often to northern medical schools and hospitals, for their practical education.

By the latter part of the century, the mounting pressures to offer opportunities for clinical work at the University had left a series of marks on the grounds. In addition to the infirmary, the Anatomical Theater was converted in 1886 to a dispensary in which medical students and faculty treated locals on an outpatient basis. Another structure for the same purpose, built on the site now occupied by the George Rogers Clark monument, opened in 1892 and provided the medical students the opportunity for clinical work. Finally, the first pavilion of the Hospital, the tiny seed that would eventually sprout into the massive medical complex, opened in 1901.

38. Old University Hospital and McKim Hall

Old University Hospital
  Paul Pelz, 1899–1901, 1904–1905, 1906–1907; several later additions by others
McKim Hall *Architectural Commission, 1930–1931*

The original University Hospital was on the west side of the old Medical School Building. Parallel to the East Range and planned as a series of linked pavilions, the structure picked up on the alignment and composition of Jefferson's original complex. The hospital and the East Range formed two sides of a large court, later terminated at the south end by the addition of Cobb Hall. Paul Pelz, best known as the designer of the Library of Congress in Washington, DC, and locally known as the architect of nearby Randall Hall, prepared the plans. The Clinical Department wing now hides Pelz's work.

The hospital and its early additions, like much of the architecture in the University Beautiful period in the first half of the twentieth century, presented thoroughly modern facilities dressed in familiar garb. The modular arrangement physically recalled Jefferson's work: each wing was tellingly described as a "pavilion." The modular system, easily expandable, accommodated construction in phases. In fact, only the central unit was built initially. Like Randall Hall, the restless massing and the detailing of the red brick buildings were more Victorian than Jeffersonian. Nonetheless, contemporaries saw the building as being in harmony with those of the Academical Village, describing Pelz's work as "colonial."

Although the medical complex has mushroomed in the later twenti-

Old University Hospital, 1899-1901, 1904-1905, 1906-1907, Paul Pelz

eth century, the initial growth was slow. Dr. Paul Barringer, the dynamic chairman of the faculty from 1896 to 1903, provided the driving force to create the hospital. When lack of funds brought the initial building campaign to a halt with only the foundation dug, the gaping hole, which stood full of water for a year, was nicknamed "Paul's Frog Pond." The setback was only temporary. By 1907, the central pavilion was finished, and both the north and south pavilions had been added. The Steele wing, designed by Walter Dabney Blair and still visible as the western wing of the old Medical School building to the north, opened in 1916. Noted University philanthropist Paul McIntire funded a similar, but not identical, addition to the south in 1924. Today the later Barringer wing conceals the McIntire wing. A 1923 master plan for the medical facilities by Fiske Kimball projected a pattern of expansion loosely modeled on the Jefferson precedent, a series of linked pavilions organized around a central open court. His dainty, formal Beaux-Arts scheme was no match for the dizzying rate of growth soon unleashed. By the early 1940s a series of later additions, including the West Addition, which now houses private clinics, buried the diminutive string of pavilions behind a wall of Jeffersonian Revival in the Georgian mode. While the restrained style of this addition differed from Pelz's work, the descriptions were hauntingly familiar. Contemporaries, like their predecessors around the turn of the century, claimed that the west addition was in the Jefferson tradition. By 1929, the University Hospital had begun to turn its back on the Grounds. An alternate entry from Jefferson Park Avenue minimized the importance of the access from the Hospital Drive. The continued growth on the landlocked site prompted University officials to consider building a wholly new facility on the North Grounds. The staggering cost quieted their enthusiasm, and, instead, many more additions were patched on to the maze of old buildings. The expanded labyrinth of buildings still serves the Health Sciences Center.

To the south is McKim Hall, built as a dormitory for the students in the nursing program. Nursing training had begun at the University in 1901. The building name honors the major donor, Dr. Randolph McKim. The style of the 1930–1931 structure, a Jeffersonian-Georgian mix, is similar to that of the Monroe Hill dormitories, also by the Architectural Commission and completed at about the same time.

39. Cobb Hall *Walter Dabney Blair, 1915–1917*

Cobb Hall, completed in 1917, housed the new chemical laboratory. The temple-fronted brick structure, now overshadowed by the health sciences center, occupied a site east of McKim, Mead & White's earlier Rouss Hall. Cobb Hall joined the hospital in expanding the University to the east of the

Cobb Hall, 1915–1917, Walter Dabney Blair

Academical Village in the early decades of the twentieth century. The building was largely the gift of J. B. Cobb, who was also one of the donors of the McConnell monument.

    The architect of Cobb Hall, Walter Dabney Blair, was well known at the University and in Charlottesville. Born in Richmond, Blair arrived at the University in 1893 and saw the return to Jeffersonian classicism in Fayerweather Hall, Carpenter and Peebles's ringing endorsement of "the lines laid down by Jefferson." After graduation, Blair continued his studies at the University of Pennsylvania and later at the École des Beaux-Arts in Paris. He designed a 1916 addition to the University Hospital, the Steele wing, and in 1919–22, the McIntire Public Library. By the early 1920s, Blair

was a member of the University's Architectural Commission, which provided most of the architecture and planning for the grounds into the 1930s.
Prior to the formation of the Board, Blair's projects for the University, such
as Cobb Hall, were solo performances.

The institutional needs and visions codified in Warren Manning's
1908 and 1913 master plans for the University determined the placement of
Cobb Hall. The north-facing Cobb Hall was intended to close the south end
of a new, long quadrangle parallel to the Academical Village. The Hospital,
with its anticipated expansion, would have solidified the eastern edge of the
narrow court. The proposed quadrangle mimicked the plan of the Jefferson
campus but acknowledged needs unknown to Jefferson. A curving artery,
proposed in 1908, became a rigid axis leading to the chemical laboratory in
1913. As finally built, Cobb Hall, like the nearby Rotunda, was the focal point
of a large outdoor room. However, unlike the Lawn and revealing the growing force that traffic needs exerted on University planning, the new quadrangle contained a road, which terminated visually in Cobb Hall.

Just as Cobb Hall's placement was molded to suit early-twentieth-
century planning priorities at the University, its appearance was in line with
turn-of-the-century notions about the appropriate style for the buildings of
the University. To harmonize the new building with those of the Jefferson
campus, Blair used the slope of the site to make the three-story building
appear as a two-story structure. Gesturing faintly to Jefferson, Blair
designed the building in a bolder, grander version of classicism reminiscent of McKim, Mead & White's work at the south end of the Lawn. As at
Cabell Hall, symmetrical brick wings flanked the building's pedimented Ionic
portico. The central entry of Cobb Hall opened into a large hall intended to
function, like Brooks Museum, as a museum dedicated to science.

The design of the new chemical laboratory also responded to
changes within the University at the turn of the century. The growing student population, the increasing emphasis on the sciences in the curriculum,
and Alderman's endorsement of practical education increased the number
of chemistry students. The larger enrollment strained the existing academic
facilities in Miller Hall, the "Old Chemical Laboratory." Just as the Old
Chemical Laboratory had been placed near the early medical building, the
Anatomical Theater, Cobb Hall was conveniently located near the
University's first hospital. Cobb Hall not only provided needed academic
space but also accommodated changing instructional methods. Prior to
1907, the University taught chemistry through lecture courses. The pressure
to provide students hands-on laboratory work required a new type of facility, met temporarily by modifying existing buildings, but later, more perma-
nently, by the construction of Cobb Hall.

Just as growth of the University had necessitated the construction
of Cobb Hall, continued development brought more changes. Planned to
accommodate future expansion, the building was enlarged in the early

1930s by the University's Architectural Commission. In the 1960s the department moved to the new Chemistry Building in the science and engineering complex on McCormick Road. Absorbed by the expanding medical facilities, Cobb Hall has been reconfigured on the interior to house several departments associated with the health sciences center. At the south end of Hospital Drive, the Chain Gate marked the entrance to the Grounds from the Fry Springs Road, now Jefferson Park Avenue. Like the Senff Gates, these simple entrance markers were the gift of Mrs. Charles Senff. Completed in 1916, the gates were designed by Blair. To the east, at the corner of Jefferson Park Avenue and Lane Road stands the lively 1896 Queen Anne Barringer Mansion. The former home of Dr. Paul Barringer is now the French House.

40. McLeod Hall, Jordan Hall, Health Sciences Library, and University Hospital

McLeod Hall *Williams and Tazewell and Associates, 1969–1972*
Jordan Hall *Baskervill and Son, 1968–1972*
Health Sciences Library *Caudill Rowlett Scott with Williams and Tazewell, 1971–1976*
University Hospital *Metcalf with Davis, Brody and Russo & Sonder, 1987–1989*

The continued expansion of the University medical facilities in the late 1960s carried the Health Sciences Center across Jefferson Park Avenue into the residential neighborhood formerly outside the grounds. Many of the large, multi-story office buildings display Modern designers' fascination with efficient and flexible interiors. The spartan detailing and the crisp blocky forms are characteristic of the numerous variations on Modern themes that marked University architecture during the Campus Suburban period (1950–c. 1976). The pervasive use of brick was the fragile thread that bound the new buildings to the traditional architecture of the grounds. Several of the most recent works shun concrete in favor of brick alone, and display stock details drawn from contemporary corporate postmodern architecture.

At 202 Fifteenth Street SW, McLeod Hall houses nursing education.

University Hospital, 1987–1989, Metcalf with Davis, Brody

Designed by Williams and Tazewell, the structure opened in 1972. The name honors Josephine McLeod, superintendent of the school of nursing from 1924 to 1937. The careful diagramming on the exterior of the building's internal functions displays a favored Modernist ordering scheme. The elevator shaft and services, the stair towers, and the large auditorium occupy prismatic volumes, broken out from the neutral backdrop of the office block beyond. Only the brick and white trim proclaim an affinity to the Jefferson vocabulary. Along Lane Road are two recent brick office and research buildings with postmodern overtones. On the north is RTKL's 1995 Jordan Hall addition. On the south is the Medical Research Building constructed in four stages; HDR and Company designed the façade and the final phase, completed in 1989.

On Jefferson Park Avenue, Jordan Hall serves as the new home of the medical school. Opened in 1972 and designed by Baskervill and Son, the severe brick box is relieved only by bands of unarticulated, horizontal windows. Lacking a sense of place, the anonymous building would be at home in any office park. The building name honors Harvey E. Jordan, the former dean of the medical school. Across the street is the towering 1960 building by Baskervill and Son, with Hankings and Anderson, which formerly housed the University Hospital. Now called the Multistory Building, the structure stretched the limits of Georgian revival vocabulary at the time it was built.

The innovative Health Sciences Library and Information Center cleverly solved a range of design problems. The building brought together at one central location the formerly scattered collection of the Health Sciences Library. Deftly linking old to new, the structure bypassed the problematic pedestrian-vehicular interface by spanning the busy thoroughfare below. Designed by Caudill Rowlett Scott, also the architects of Ruffner Hall, the structure opened in 1976. Like McLeod Hall, the Hospital Link is an abstract composition of simple geometric forms, executed in the University's traditional palette. The Hospital Link beyond provides a similar above-grade connection between old and new.

The main recent addition to the complex is the new University Hospital by Metcalf with Davis, Brody and Russo & Sonder. The gleaming, faceted tower rests lightly on the building's base, predictably sheathed in brick. Highly visible, the white aluminum panels form a sleek, clinical skin that speaks the antiseptic language of the contents at the expense of the language of the context.

41. Stacey Hall *Stevens and Wilkinson, 1957*

Stacey Hall is a rare example—in Charlottesville—of Modern architecture poured from the Miesian mold. Built to house a local Sears Roebuck and Co. store, the structure opened in 1957. At that time, it was the largest retail store in the city. Instead of a traditional façade facing the street, the building presented identical faces to West Main Street and to the all-important parking lot, whose prominent presence offered evidence of the increasing numbers of patrons that arrived by auto. The thin wall of glass was made possible by freeing the thermal barrier from its traditional load-bearing responsibilities. The large sheets of glazing maximized the amount of display space. The colonnade of I-beams, a direct quotation from Ludwig Mies van der Rohe's work at the Illinois Institute of Technology, supported a frieze of metal panels. The porch sheltered the banks of windows, which were held lightly in narrow metal frames. North of the parking lot, the garage doors, now infilled, provided access to the automotive wing. The architects, Stevens and Wilkinson, an Atlanta firm with a regional practice, designed a number of stores for the well-known national company in the 1950s. Each, in an appropriately Modern vocabulary, actively promoted the company's progressive image.

The University acquired the building in 1982, after Sears left West Main Street to move to Fashion Square Mall. Renamed to honor John M. Stacey, the former director of the University Hospital and the first director of the Medical Center, the structure now contains office, academic, and medical research space. The University has protected and enhanced the Miesian qualities of this delicate period piece of commercial architecture.

42. Corner Building *Eugene Bradbury, 1912–1914*

The transformation of the area around the Corner Building and the Senff Gates illustrates, in microcosm, the changing institutional priorities at the University in the nineteenth and twentieth centuries. What began as an essentially utilitarian zone containing professors' gardens in the early nineteenth century gradually became a main entry to the reoriented and stylisti-

Corner Building, 1912–1914, Eugene Bradbury

cally homogenized grounds. The much-criticized Temperance Hall and the "Old Corner" disappeared under a broadly brushed Jeffersonesque wash, applied early in the twentieth century. Within a decade and a half, the explosive growth of the medical school swept away part of this refined and delicate gilding at the east entrance to make way for the new, showy, and monumental home of the school of medicine.

In the mid-nineteenth century prior to the construction of the Corner Building, the now-shady site was a battleground of wills. To some members of the University community, the ragged commercial district known as the Corner, which was outside the boundaries and control of the University, afforded a mixed blessing. It offered not only support but also temptation to the students of the Academical Village. The two-story brick Temperance Hall, a contemporary of the Rotunda Annex and the Infirmary, was a rectangular building of mixed architectural pedigree: an arcade of wall arches at the first floor supported the second-floor engaged pilasters, which carried a corbel table above. But the modest building packed a moral punch. Pointedly positioned on University property opposite the source of the problem, the structure defiantly challenged the establishments such as a nearby "grog-shop." Temperance Hall was intended to be a stirring symbol and the local propaganda arm of a forceful nineteenth-century reform movement, supported by local luminaries such as Board of Visitors member and Bremo owner John Hartwell Cocke and by noted law professor John B. Minor. After the temperance movement lost momentum later in the nineteenth century, the University refashioned its physical home for other uses. In the early twentieth century, it housed a bookstore and the post office.

The gentrification of the area in the early twentieth century swept away the by-then perceived as "unsightly" Temperance Hall and spilled over onto the Corner. The Corner Building, an exuberant neo-Jeffersonian structure, originally called the Entrance Building, replaced the dour Temperance Hall. A similar impulse motivated the demolition of several "wooden shanties" to make way for the elaborate and substantial brick Chancellor Building on the Corner. Designed by local architect Bradbury, the Corner building, housed the post office and shops, including a tearoom, in a refined envelope that drank from roots sunk deep into the local tradition. The structure that the Board of Visitors hoped would produce "larger revenues and a better appearance of the entrance to the University," a contemporary critic described as "a dignified building in keeping with the architectural style of Jefferson." Bradbury was well known locally for his Colonial Revival work. The new entrance gates at the lower end of the "Long Walk" originally figured in part of his project and appeared in the rendering of the proposed building. At Alderman's insistence, Henry Bacon redesigned the Senff Gates, which were the focal point of the vehicular path from Charlottesville and the embellished threshold between town and gown.

The Corner Building, an early product of the Alderman years, survived the growth of the campus during the mature period of his presidency but only because of a change of site. To make way for the Medical School Building, the Corner Building was relocated—body first, columns second—to its present site, further east on University Avenue. The Corner Building presently houses the Women's Center and other University administrative offices and programs.

43. Medical School Building

Coolidge, Shepley, Bulfinch and Abbott, 1926–1929

The construction of the Medical School Building gave the medical department a grand, prominent, and highly visible home on the grounds. The new structure reorganized and reoriented the University's medical facilities. The academic building for the medical program brought together, in a single location, the preclinical classes that had been formerly scattered across the grounds. Prior to the construction of the Medical School Building, the original hospital consisted of a chain of linked pavilions parallel to and facing the East Range. The northernmost of the hospital pavilions, the Steele wing, with its engaged Ionic colonnade on the north elevation, set the tone for the new construction. The Boston architects of the Medical School Building,

Medical School Building, 1926–1929, Coolidge, Shepley, Bulfinch and Abbott

Coolidge, Shepley, Bulfinch and Abbott, duplicated the north elevation of the Steele wing, with only minor variations, on the opposite side of the new pedimented entry portico. The entrance to the Medical School was just inside the Senff Gates, an imposing portal accessed from the grounds. The new outpatient entry, from Jefferson Park Avenue, was pointedly positioned outside the walls. In 1923, Fiske Kimball had suggested a very different scheme for the expansion of the medical facilities. He, too, had relocated the entrance to the north but had reused the existing Entrance [Corner] Building on its original site as the main entry to the proposed complex. By contrast, the even grander late-1920s solution relocated the Corner Building.

Facing the Corner, the Medical School Building was a large U-shaped complex, physically attached at two points to the existing hospital and open to the east. The massive portico and the wing east of it formed the northern arm of the new structure. Like the nearly contemporary Memorial Gymnasium, the structure presented a grand reinterpretation of the Jeffersonian vocabulary—deferential, but just barely so. The architects partly disguised the building's enormous size by using the slope of the site. Although the materials and classical detailing pointed to Jefferson, the façade, with grand colonnades of engaged three-quarter columns resting on the high basements, recalled a large government building. The central hexastyle portico makes obvious reference to that of the Rotunda. The columns are respectfully shorter than those of the model, but only by two feet. That the medical school's portico opens into a handsome circular lobby should not be a surprise. Although the lobby plan recalls Jefferson, the heavy and shaded space contrasts sharply with the buoyant, light-filled Dome Room of the Rotunda nearby.

The Medical School Building's bold presence celebrated the resolution of a protracted controversy. The University's rural setting had long been used as a weapon to question the wisdom of funding a large state-supported medical facility in Charlottesville. The push to consolidate the state's medical training into a single school in Richmond resurfaced in the early twentieth century. In 1912, even President Alderman, as chair of a Virginia Education Commission, supported the relocation of the University's medical school to the capital city. However, by the early 1920s, he saw the move differently and campaigned vigorously to keep the medical school in Charlottesville. Alderman and the University celebrated the defeat of the bill proposing consolidation as a personal and institutional triumph. The construction of the Medical School Building later in the same decade firmly and indelibly stamped the sealed decision with a heavy masonry pile.

Until the completion of Jordan Hall in the 1970s, the medical school remained in its imposing quarters opposite the Corner. Other additions have followed until the accretive pile has become a tangle of alterations and renovations. Today the original Medical School Building houses office, research, laboratory, and clinical facilities.

Rugby Road and Carr's Hill

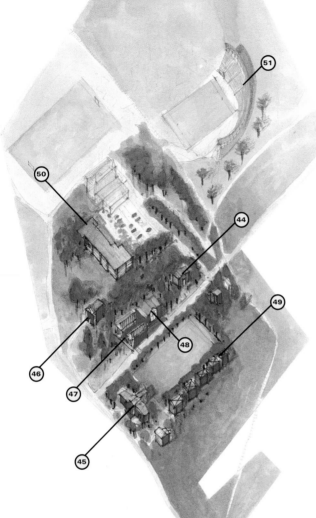

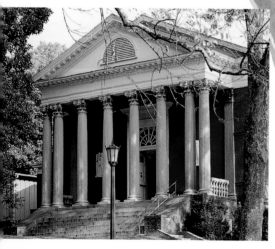

The Grounds
Expand to the North

The Rugby Road and Carr's Hill walk explores the mix of buildings located north of University Avenue. Prior to the Civil War, campus growth had clung to the perimeter of the Academical Village. After the war, the University transformed the farmland north of the Rotunda with buildings and infrastructure to accommodate expansion. The resulting fabric— housing, playing fields, institutional buildings, and a strip of commercial structures at the Corner—functioned as support facilities for the grounds.

The walk contains works by a number of notable University-employed architects. The President's House on Carr's Hill by McKim, Mead & White is a paradigm of Southern Colonial Revival design. John Kevan Peebles's stunning Fayerweather Hall signaled the return to the Jefferson tradition that would dominate the design of University buildings until the 1960s. In less than 20 years, the tentative appliqué of classicism on Fayerweather Hall became a powerful classical vision, extending out across the landscape in R. E. Lee Taylor's Lambeth Colonnade. Still later in the twentieth century, Pietro Belluschi and Kenneth DeMay brought Modern architecture to Carr's Hill in their design of the initial phase of the fine arts complex.

The walk begins at the commercial district known as the Corner. To the west, along University Avenue, is Carr's Hill, crowned by the President's House but also home to a number of early-twentieth-century fraternity houses and the still-incomplete fine arts complex. On Rugby Road, opposite the University art museum, a number of the fraternity— and now also sorority—houses appear across Madison Bowl. The Lambeth Colonnade, today an evocative ruin, at the transformed Lambeth Field area marks the terminus of the walk.

Lambeth Field, 1901–1902. Lambeth Colonnade, 1911–13, R. E. Lee Taylor

44. The Corner and St. Paul's Memorial Church

St. Paul's Memorial Church   *Eugene Bradbury, 1925–1927*

The Corner

"The Corner" constituted the commercial foil to Jefferson's self-contained academic community. Since Jefferson had purposefully isolated his University from Charlottesville, the Corner developed to serve the Academical Village and to supplement the spartan lifestyle housed in the original complex. Commercial establishments as well as boardinghouses and churches contributed to the accretive growth near the University in the nineteenth century. Private enterprise rather than institutional planning guided the growth. The buildings are not officially part of the University.

The Corner grew along well-traveled transportation routes. The initial armature of roads around which the district developed predated the University. The roads today known as University Avenue and West Main Street connected the University to Charlottesville. Originally they were part of the Three Notch'd Road, a colonial highway that linked Richmond with the Shenandoah Valley. The Three Notch'd Road, sometimes also called the Three Chopt Road, took its name from the three notches or "chops" emblazoned on trees to mark the path. Railroads, which arrived in the mid-nineteenth century, also left a mark on the landscape near the University. The district begins at Jefferson Park Avenue, the old road south to Lynchburg.

Although the Corner developed in response to the needs of the University, the planning patterns of the two were entirely different. Jefferson's formal, hierarchical, rational plan for the Academical Village was prepared in advance and the finished composition then overlaid on the irregular landscape. By contrast, the Corner grew slowly in a piecemeal, ad hoc, less formal manner, always in response to the needs of the University across the street. A few businesses existed in the 1830s along the Three Notch'd Road northeast of the University. As the enrollment nearly quadrupled from 1900 to 1930, the University built few additional dormitories, and student housing remained inadequate. The construction of boardinghouses on and near the Corner, to make room for the additional students, dovetailed with the construction of fraternity houses nearby. The steadily increasing enrollment and the growth of the University to the north fueled the construction of commercial facilities at the Corner. The earlier lightly scattered businesses

St. Paul's Memorial Church, 1925–1927,
Eugene Bradbury

became a solid strip of service build-ings during the late nineteenth and early twentieth centuries.

Notable buildings remain. The Chancellor Building at 1411–1415 University Avenue opened c. 1916 to house Chancellor's Drug Store. Contrasting decorative limestone at the entablature, window lintels, and the broken Doric frieze, which sepa-rates the first and second floors, orna-ment the handsome commercial structure. The arcaded storefront in the west unit is original. The most striking building on the Corner is the former Anderson Brothers Bookstore at 1417–1425 University Avenue. The 1848 two-story brick building was enlarged in the 1890s and the elaborate pressed metal facade by J. K. Mesker Co. of St. Louis installed. Engaged Composite colonnettes flank the window bays at the upper floors. The facade, assembled on site, was modular, ornate, and relatively easy to erect. The finished product typified American commercial architecture of the period. The c.1925 Stevens-Shepherd building, now Starbucks Coffee, at 1601 University Avenue is neo-Georgian. For most of its life, the build-ing housed department stores. Immediately west of the commercial dis-trict, Eugene Bradbury's St. Paul's Memorial Church at 1700 University Avenue is a Georgian revival ecclesiastical building in the tradition of McKim, Mead & White's work for the University across the street. Next door is the Federal revival Booker House, built as a boardinghouse c. 1905 and in operation until 1967. The splayed window lintels with projecting keystones, the elliptical fanlight and sidelights at the entry, and the attenu-ated Doric columns on the portico make reference to the architecture of the early republic.

45. Madison Hall *Parish and Schroeder, 1904–1905*

Madison Hall, located directly across University Avenue from the Rotunda, originally housed the nation's oldest chapter of the Young Men's Christian Association. During the nineteenth century, the lengthy debate over the role of religion in the life of the University generated a series of proposals for a chapel on the grounds. Similar concerns also led to the 1858 founding at the University of Virginia of the first American college chapter of the YMCA.

Madison Hall, 1904–1905,
Parish and Schroeder

Madison Hall gave this organization a physical home in a prominent location adjacent to the grounds.

Joining Fayerweather Gymnasium, Madison Hall formed part of the expansion of the University and its associated activities to the north during the University Beautiful period of the first half of the twentieth century. Madison Hall was a Beaux-Arts-inspired Georgian-Jeffersonian conflation that contemporaries often described as colonial. The use of brick and the appliqué of classical details tied the new building to the vocabulary of the existing campus. Earlier twentieth-century projects, such as Fayerweather Gymnasium and the old Hospital, displayed a Victorian formal busyness: the active profile accompanied a composition made up of many smaller pieces. By contrast, the serene, dignified massing, the simplified profile, and the hierarchically ordered three-part facade used at Madison Hall became a formula applied to many of the later University buildings, such as Cobb and Peabody Halls.

Madison Hall brought together distinguished names from the University community and a firm noted for its design of educational buildings. Parish and Schroeder of New York served as the architects, and Mrs. William E. Dodge of New York City donated the funds for the building's construction. The building's name honored former United States President James Madison, who had succeeded Jefferson as rector. A former student of the University, Woodrow Wilson, delivered the address at the dedication of Madison Hall in 1905.

Changing priorities at the University have generated a series of subsequent uses for Madison Hall. The building housed YMCA activities until the 1930s. The University leased the building for use as a student

Madison Bowl and Madison Lane Fraternity Houses

union in the 1940s before purchasing Madison Hall in 1971. Since 1984, the structure has contained administrative offices, including those of the University president.

Behind Madison Hall, to the north, is Madison Bowl, a sunken athletic playing field, known locally as "Mad Bowl." Although the origins of the rectangular depression are unknown, the area had been graded and used for athletics prior to the 1895 Rotunda fire. The site was part of the YMCA's property when it had Madison Hall built. Tennis courts owned and operated by the Association occupied the site until the 1930s. The University acquired "Mad Bowl" in 1971 at the same time that it purchased Madison Hall. The playing field now accommodates University intramural sports.

East of Madison Bowl, along Madison Lane, a collection of University fraternity and sorority houses forms the lively backdrop to the activity field below. Red brick and white-columned porticoes on many of the houses, built between 1902 and 1928, provide the unity that binds numerous variations on the Colonial revival theme into a harmonious whole. A housing shortage prior to the construction of the Monroe Hill dormitories in the late 1920s and the desire of the social clubs to own their own housing prompted the construction of fraternity houses on or near the campus beginning around 1900. The nearby athletic facilities and the YMCA formed the nucleus that attracted the fraternities to join the expansion of the University to the north. Following the admission of women to the University in 1970, sororities purchased and moved into some of the houses on Madison Lane.

46. Carr's Hill *McKim, Mead & White, 1906–1909*

Carr's Hill, the residence of the University president and an exemplary early-twentieth-century design of the University Beautiful period, transformed an existing motley assemblage of buildings on the site. In the late nineteenth century, student housing had dotted Carr's Hill, which takes its name from Mrs. Sidney Carr, one of the private mid-nineteenth-century boarding-house operators. The University purchased Carr's Hill in 1867; a fire that same year destroyed most of these early buildings. The University replaced the structures with institutionally operated housing. Several remnants of the nineteenth-century occupation of Carr's Hill survive. One of the oldest and smallest is the

Carr's Hill

Carr's Hill gardens and the guest house

ironically named Buckingham Palace. Although its origins are obscure, the brick, gable-roofed structure with a corbelled brick cornice was most likely built as student lodging shortly after 1856. To the north, behind the president's house, the two-story brick gable-roofed structure with a double verandah is the one surviving unit of a set of dormitories the University built shortly after the fire. It is now used as guest quarters. The Leake Cottage, a single-story brick building, is a fragment of the dining hall built by the University in 1888 to serve the student housing complex. A portion of this building was demolished at the time of the construction of the President's house. The remaining portion now houses offices. Today, components from both the nineteenth- and twentieth-century uses co-exist on Carr's Hill.

The elegant two-story brick President's House crowns the small hill south of the Academical Village and overlooks a sweeping park-like lawn. University Avenue and the Central Grounds are beyond. The gardens range in design from the formal parterres on the north to the expansive shaded lawn on the south. Stanford White, of the New York firm McKim, Mead & White, prepared the original sketches for the house. After White's sensational murder in June 1906, his firm redesigned the building, which was completed in 1909. McKim, Mead & White also designed the c. 1908 carriage house.

The construction of the President's House played a role in the sweeping institutional changes at the University at the turn of the century. Like the new buildings at the south end of the Lawn, the President's House figured in the rebirth of the University in the wake of the Rotunda fire. Creating the new position of a university president signaled a departure from Jefferson's looser administrative organization. Carr's Hill gave the new administrator a grand and dignified presence on the University grounds. The placement on top of a small hill adjacent to the Academical Village suited the hierarchical significance of the new building.

The typical description of the style of Carr's Hill as Colonial Revival is doubly misleading. The President's House, like other McKim, Mead & White Colonial Revival residences in the late nineteenth and early twentieth centuries, does not literally imitate a colonial building. And while Jefferson's work at the University is the point of departure, the Jefferson campus—built in the nineteenth century—is hardly colonial. The pedimented portico and the tympanum lunette do come out of the Jefferson tradition. However, the enormous size of the residence, the elliptical fanlight and traceried sidelights at the entry, the fluted columns, and the elaborate window trim at both floors depart from the Jefferson idiom while massaging the memory to create a prestigious image. Carr's Hill, with its graceful garden setting, creates an impression of refined, comfortable elegance that draws on the myth of the Old South recalled in much of the Southern Colonial Revival architecture of the period.

47. Fayerweather Hall   *Carpenter and Peebles, 1892–1893*

Fayerweather Gymnasium, now Fayerweather Hall, is the University's oldest surviving purpose-built sports facility. Jefferson had made no provision for athletics beyond the designation of the spaces in the arcades on the south side of the Rotunda as exercise areas. Mid-nineteenth-century students organized informal associations to fund and maintain various

Fayerweather Hall

collections of equipment on the grounds. The gymnasium and baths by J. E. D'Alfonce and William Pratt and the renovation of Hotel F as the Squibb Gymnasium offered temporary solutions. By contrast, substantial Fayerweather Gymnasium answered the need for an appropriate sports center to house activities associated with the rising interest in intercollegiate athletics. Like the function, the architectural style also marked a departure. The designers claimed to have reintroduced Jeffersonian Roman classicism to the University. In reality, they had appropriated and transformed the elements of the Jeffersonian vocabulary to suit an entirely new function. The materials of the two-story red brick "temple to sweat" echoed those of the Lawn, but motifs such as the rusticated brick base had no antecedent in Jefferson's work. The pedimented portico at the entry is reminiscent of those on Jefferson's pavilions and Rotunda, but the attenuated, fluted columns are not. These fragments of the familiar, borrowed from the founder's vocabulary, screened the unfamiliar, the unprecedented size of the gymnasium within. Successive reworkings of the Jeffersonian idiom, which dominated University architecture until the 1960s, trace their roots to this building.

The design of Fayerweather brought a new patron and a new architect to the University. The project was one of a series of gymnasia that were funded by wealthy New York shoe manufacturer Daniel B. Fayerweather for campuses across the country. Norfolk architects Carpenter and Peebles designed this gymnasium. John Kevan Peebles, an 1890 Virginia graduate, remained an influential voice in the design of University architecture until his death in 1934; Fayerweather was his first project here. In an 1894 article in *Alumni Bulletin* promoting his firm's design of the gymnasium, Peebles claimed, "While no copy of any classic structure . . . [it] follows the lines laid down by Jefferson." He also argued for the rehabilitation of Jefferson's place in the history as the architect of the University. Reinforcing this position, Fayerweather Gymnasium presented a return to the Jefferson architectural tradition. The style emphatically rejected the Victorian eclecticism of the chapel and Brooks Hall.

Although Peebles promoted Fayerweather as "a thing of beauty, a joy forever" at the time it was built, the modest structure soon became outdated. Memorial Gymnasium replaced it in 1924, and Fayerweather was remodeled to accommodate the McIntire School of Fine Arts. Wealthy stockbroker Paul Goodloe McIntire was a former student at the University and later a member of the Board of Visitors. In addition to his endowment of the commerce school and his funding of the McIntire Amphitheater, he provided the gift to found the McIntire School of Fine Arts in 1919. The University named architect and noted architectural historian Fiske Kimball as the school's first professor of art. With the athletic functions installed in Memorial Gymnasium, the art school moved in 1924 to Fayerweather from its quarters in Hotel E. When the architecture school moved to

Campbell Hall in 1970, Fayerweather Hall became the home of the McIntire Department of Art.

Minor touches have altered the exterior of the building. After the school of fine arts moved in, the Victorian florid ornaments in the pediment were removed and replaced by a new tympanum lunette that came straight out of the Jefferson vocabulary. The pavilions at the second floor on the east originally flanked an open balustraded gallery, which overlooked the activities in Madison Bowl below. Today, a wall penetrated by a line of ocular windows encloses the gallery.

48. Bayly Art Museum *Edmund S. Campbell and R. E. Lee Taylor, 1933–1935*

The designers of the Bayly Art Museum wove Renaissance motifs into the Jefferson vocabulary to enhance the monumentality of the University's first art museum. In a manner similar to Jefferson's treatment of the Rotunda, the entablature of the porch wraps around the building below the top of the wall to bind the entry to the rectangular block of the building behind. While the slightly projecting end pavilions on the facade loosely recall Jefferson's work, the blind windows at their centers are Renaissance motifs that also indicate the light-sensitive contents within. The metal grilles at the windows announce that the contents are valuable and are reminiscent of the treatment of the ground floor windows of Renaissance palazzi. The dominant element of the facade, the monumental pedimented porch, contains a wholly un-Jeffersonian Serliana, a favorite Palladian motif composed of an arched opening flanked by a pair of narrower linteled openings. The architects' reinterpretation of the Jefferson legacy follows in the tradition of McKim, Mead & White. The reference to the late Renaissance work of Palladio carried associations of refinement and sophistication, which identified the Bayly as a cultural institution.

Both the building and the site are stamped with images and events from the University's past. The museum honored Thomas H. Bayly and was largely the gift of Mrs. Evelyn May Bayly Tiffany. A PWA grant supplemented her bequest. Like Thornton Hall and Alderman Library, the museum is one of several fruits of New Deal funding that dot the grounds. The designers, as members of the Architectural Commission, had an innate regard for University

Bayly Art Museum

tradition. Campbell, a teaching architect, headed the art and architecture program from 1927 to 1950. Taylor's other work at the University included the design of the Lambeth Colonnade and of Alderman Library. The construction of the art museum necessitated the demolition of the house that the University had built next to Fayerweather Gymnasium for the multi-talented director of athletics, William A. Lambeth.

Placing the Bayly Museum on a site adjacent to the art school's new home in Fayerweather Hall established the nucleus of an arts complex on Carr's Hill. The building housed the department's art collection, which consisted of donations both from Mrs. Tiffany and the department's major benefactor, Paul Goodloe McIntire. However, growth of the school soon pushed expansion into the museum. By 1962, the architecture program occupied the entire building. Following the opening of new facilities for the school of architecture in the early 1970s, the building was renovated and reopened in 1974 as a museum.

49. Carr's Hill Fraternity Houses *1908–1928*

The large number of fraternity houses on and near Carr's Hill reveals the importance of such social organizations in the life of the University during the late nineteenth and early twentieth centuries. Like the growth of athletics, the rise of fraternities in Charlottesville paralleled a national trend. The earliest fraternities on the grounds were social rather than residential organizations. By the early twentieth century, the shortage of student housing led to the construction of residential chapter houses on or near the grounds. The expansion of the campus to the north, which had brought Fayerweather Gymnasium, Lambeth Field, and the YMCA in Madison Hall to the Rugby Road area, as well as the availability of land, attracted the fraternities to the lots nearby.

The University fraternities built houses on both private and university-owned sites. Delta Psi completed the first purpose-built chapter house, known as Saint Anthony Hall, on a site between Madison Lane and Chancellor Street, in 1902. A number of fraternities followed their lead by building houses on Madison Lane, Rugby Road, and other nearby locations prior to 1930. To encourage as well as to control the growth, the University allocated space for fraternity houses on Carr's Hill. The University mandated that their style be in keeping with the other campus structures. The houses are a collection of Georgian-Jeffersonian revival buildings, typical of the work at the University during this period. The 1913 master plan by Boston landscape architect Warren Manning guided the placement, indicating sites for seven fraternity houses on Carr's Hill. The formal fraternity quadrangle on Rugby Road was executed essentially as Manning had planned. Each of the houses is Georgian Revival. Ludlow and Peabody's Delta Tau Delta, now Sigma Phi, occupies the site at the head of "Fraternity Court." The 1911 structure is one of the most elaborate of the University's chapter houses. A colossal semicircular Tuscan portico, which engages an enclosed porch at the first floor, marks the central entry on the axis of the court. James L. Burley's 1908–11 Kappa Sigma house forms the north side of the quadrangle. A central Ionic portico marks the entry to the three-story, hipped-roof brick structure. Eugene Bradbury's 1922 Chi Phi House, on the opposite side of the court, displays a variation on the same theme.

The most striking of the Carr's Hill fraternity houses is Louis Voorhees's 1924–26 Zeta Psi house. One-story wings, with semi-octagonal ends, flank the two-story central block of the brick house. A Doric, tetrastyle pedimented portico marks the central entry. The most literally Jeffersonian of the Carr's Hill fraternity houses, the cruciform plan building was based on the pre-1772 version of Monticello. The two other fraternity houses on Carr's Hill Road—now Culbreth Road—loosely conform to Manning's placement. The austere 1914 Delta Kappa Epsilon, set on a sloping site on the west side of Carr's Hill, houses the University's oldest fraternity. Next door is Louis Justement's imaginatively sited 1927–28 Sigma Nu house. The semicircular Ionic front portico, set on a rusticated basement and overlooking the playing fields below, is the visual terminus to Ivy Road.

The construction of the fraternity houses between 1908 and 1928 brought a different type of resident to Carr's Hill. Like the nineteenth-century dormitories, the fraternities provided housing for students but with the added twist of sorting by social affiliation. The handsome buildings continue to serve their original function.

Carr's Hill Fraternity Houses, 1908–1928

50. Campbell Hall, Fiske Kimball Fine Arts Library, and Drama Building

Campbell Hall and Fiske Kimball Fine Arts Library

Rawlings and Wilson, with Pietro Belluschi;
Kenneth DeMay of Sasaki, Dawson, DeMay, 1965–1970

Drama Building   *Rawlings, Wilson and Fraher, 1970–1974*

The notion of a fine arts compound on Carr's Hill figured prominently in the tremendous rebuilding of the University begun under President Darden and continued under President Shannon. The University grew rapidly after World War II and more than tripled in size between 1940 and 1970. Federal funding for the sciences in the 1960s fueled the development of the science complex. The University commissioned a fine arts complex to comparably develop the arts curriculum. Campbell Hall houses a dream of the University's founder. Jefferson had included architecture within one of the schools of his University. He wrote that the principal buildings in his Academical Village would be "models of chaste architecture, as examples for the school of architecture to be formed on." The collection formed a three-dimensional set of standards for study—"specimens for the architectural lectures." Jefferson's plan for instruction in architecture at the University was finally fulfilled with the creation of the McIntire School of Fine Arts in 1919. Housed briefly in Hotel E at the end of the West Range, the program operated in the converted Fayerweather Hall and later in the Bayly Museum until the school of architecture's move to much larger quarters in Campbell Hall in 1970.

Like Jefferson's work at the Lawn, Campbell Hall clearly endorsed an architecture laden with meaning. For Jefferson, ideals of civic virtue were embedded in the Roman classical forms that he used. The dean of the architecture school Joseph N. Bosserman, who presided over the construction of Campbell Hall, asserted that it was the "most significant building constructed at the University since Jefferson designed and built the academical village, in terms of style, character, innovation, quality, and almost any other good term

Drama Building

you choose." Where Jefferson's complex was a collection of lightly scaled,
richly ornamented buildings set on a
plateau, the massive architecture building, devoid of ornament, burrowed
itself into the north side of Carr's Hill.
Jefferson's buildings—"models of good
taste and good architecture, & of a variety of appearance, no two alike . . ."—
demonstrated the richness of the classi-

Campbell Hall

cal language. It was their variety that provided the counterpoint to the overall
regularity of his complex. Rather than timeless proportions and model moldings, Campbell Hall's ornament is the student activity within, visible through
the large expanses of glass on the facade. Each of the suspended bays was a
light, hovering volume, so dear to the Modern designer's vocabulary. Like
other examples of Modern architecture, the building paid homage to the utility of engineering, materials, and structure. Still, the lingering presence of
Jefferson was felt even here. The materials were red brick with white trim,
although they were distilled into taut, angular planes and stretched over the
exposed concrete frame. The large rectangular bays that ripple across the
facade recast Jefferson's modular organization of the Academical Village as a
crisp, spartan, Modern set of forms.

Campbell Hall was planned as a single component of a large fine
arts complex. The zoning of Carr's Hill as the arts center came out of the
1965 University master plan by the influential campus planners and architects Sasaki, Dawson, DeMay Associates of Cambridge, Massachusetts. The
University subsequently hired the firm to design its new arts compound.
Pietro Belluschi collaborated with Kenneth DeMay on the project. Belluschi,
an AIA Gold medalist and dean of the School of Architecture and Planning at
MIT, was best known as the designer of the 1944–48 Equitable Building in
Portland, Oregon. The direct expression of the structural frame, the sleek
glazing, and the wholly modern relationship between solid and void of the
Equitable Building reappeared at the architecture school for Mr. Jefferson's
university. While the Sasaki, Dawson, DeMay, and Belluschi team handled
the design work, Rawlings and Wilson of Richmond, the architects of record,
produced the working drawings and provided contract administration.

The building that houses the training of architects was appropriately named to honor an architect, Edmund S. Campbell, who directed the
architecture program from 1927 to 1950. Ironically, while the building that
bears his name is assertively Modern, Campbell was a committed classicist.
In addition to his work on the Board of Architects' numerous projects in the
1920s and 1930s, Campbell also collaborated on both the design of the
Bayly Museum and an addition to Alumni Hall and was the architect of the
diminutive Lady Astor Squash Courts.

The Fiske Kimball Fine Arts Library, designed and constructed concurrently with Campbell Hall, was a product of the same team of architects. The style is similar. Like the architecture building, the library honors a luminary from the school's past. Fiske Kimball was an architect, historian, and Jefferson scholar when he was hired as the University's first professor of art and architecture. Kimball's wrote his PhD dissertation at the University of Michigan on Jefferson's Virginia State Capitol. His 1916 book, *Thomas Jefferson, Architect*, remains a classic study of Jefferson's design work. During his brief four-year stay at the University, Kimball served on the design committee for Memorial Gymnasium and was the architect of the McIntire Amphitheater and of the Faculty Apartments.

In the end, the Drama Building marked the only other portion of the arts complex executed. Although configured somewhat differently, a structure for the drama department appeared in the 1965 master plan. Completed in 1974, Rawlings, Wilson, and Fraher, without their former collaborators, designed the Drama Building. The style is in keeping with the earlier work nearby. The planned arts compound remains incomplete. Each of the buildings constructed continues to serve its original function. Currently an addition to the architecture school and a building for the music department are under consideration.

51. Lambeth Field, Lambeth Colonnade, Faculty Apartments, and Lambeth Field Apartments

Lambeth Field *1901–1902*
Lambeth Colonnade *R. E. Lee Taylor, 1911–1913*
Faculty Apartments *Fiske Kimball, 1922*
Lambeth Field Apartments
Rawlings, Wilson and Fraher with Kenneth DeMay of Sasaki, Dawson, and DeMay, 1972–1974

The Lambeth Field complex is a memento from the birth of the University's athletic program. A rising interest in organized sports accompanied the growth of the student population and campus around the turn of the century. The original Academical Village had included no dedicated athletic facilities. The need for playing fields and a structure for athletics received architectural expression in Fayerweather Gymnasium and Madison Bowl. The construction of Lambeth Field and the Colonnade between 1901 and 1913 provided facilities for football, baseball, and track in the development north of the grounds. A small valley north of Carr's Hill was chosen for the Lambeth Field project. Although unrecognized at the time, the site selection exchanged a short-term advantage for a long-term problem. The natural fall of the site required less manipulation to accommodate the seating and field. However, the natural drainage through the site has been an ongoing maintenance problem causing deterioration of the concrete. The key architectural feature of the athletic complex is a ring of concrete bleachers. Built in three stages between 1911 and 1913, the concrete seating replaced the original wooden bleachers. The elegant Doric colonnade at the top is anchored by arcaded end pavilions and capped by a red tile roof. The recasting of Jefferson's architectural vocabulary was typical of the design work in the first half of the 1900s during the University Beautiful period. Here, as at other American colleges, designers of athletic stadia frequently turned to ancient prototypes. The classical amphitheater, loosely interpreted, set the model for Lambeth Field as well as Soldiers Field at Harvard and Lewisohn Field at the City College of New York, built in the same period.

The architect for the Lambeth Colonnade was R. E. Lee Taylor. A graduate of the University, Taylor practiced in Norfolk with several firms between 1906 and 1915, prior to relocating to Baltimore. He served as a member of the Architectural Commission in the 1920s and 1930s and designed a number of University projects including Alderman Library. In addition to his architectural practice and work at the University, he served on the Advisory Committee of Architects overseeing the restoration of Colonial Williamsburg from 1927 to 1935. The stadium was named for Dr. William A. Lambeth, whose positions at the University encompassed director of athletics, professor of hygiene, and superintendent of buildings and grounds. Lambeth also wrote books on a variety of topics, including one of the first studies of Thomas Jefferson's architecture.

Although Lambeth Colonnade has been an integral component of the grounds for almost a century, the field, once the heart of the University's outdoor athletic endeavors, is a facility without a function. Despite its continuing importance as a landscape feature and its nostalgic appeal, the stadium's original functions have been dispersed to other sites. Because of the student housing inserted in the 1970s, the athletic facility is now employed for more modest scale activities: the field accommodates intramural games and informal sports, and students use the seating as a sunning and study location. Nonetheless, even in decay, the colonnade is a dramatic component of the campus landscape.

Behind the Lambeth Colonnade to the east stands a large brick structure, now faculty apartments but begun as an athletic clubhouse. Paul Pelz's plan for the clubhouse in 1903 and that of Ferguson, Calrow, and Taylor in 1915 offered different interpretations of the Jefferson architectural legacy. Although the foundations for the Ferguson, Calrow, and Taylor version were eventually laid, both proposals eventually foundered from lack of funding. Fiske Kimball reused the abandoned foundations as the substructure to support the 1922 Faculty Apartments. The faculty housing was grafted onto the roots of a very different project—the unrealized dream of an athletic clubhouse.

52 | **University Hall**
53 | **Klöckner Stadium**
54 | **Darden School**
55 | **Law School and**
     | **Judge Advocate General's School**

A Satellite Campus to Jefferson's Academical Village

The North Grounds contain buildings and landscapes associated with the University's growth in the last half of the twentieth century. Two parcels of land purchased by the University—the former Massie dairy farm and the Duke tract—house a sprawling athletic complex and a set of professional schools. After World War II and with greater speed beginning in the 1960s, the University transformed the rural landscape into a satellite campus following a suburban model of development.

By the 1970s, rapid growth strained the existing facilities on the by-then landlocked and overcrowded Central Grounds. The available land, although located at a distance from the rest of the campus, afforded a solution to the problems associated with the University's expansion. The North Grounds represented one of several satellite campuses considered to accommodate University expansion; it was the only one actually built. The University purchased the Massie estate, now the site of University Hall, in 1945 and erected the short-lived Copeley Hill student housing complex there. The acquisition of the former Duke estate in 1963 augmented the extensive holdings on Copeley Hill. The mid-nineteenth-century Gothic revival house, Sunnyside, had been the home of Col. R. T. W. Duke and is the oldest surviving building on the North Grounds. While the 1965 master plan proposed only sports facilities and student housing for the site that later became the North Grounds, the Duke tract made a remote campus possible. The increasing importance of the automobile placed new land demands on the growth. The suburban feel and the large areas of surface parking demonstrate the domineering impact of the car on the planning and design of the North Grounds. Until the 1990s, the buildings, often created by well-known designers of collegiate architecture, formed a version of modernism that gestured only faintly to Jefferson.

The walk visits artifacts from the recent development on the North Grounds. The barracks and trailers from the Copeley Hill housing, like the Massie farmhouse, are now gone. Sunnyside is University-owned but now serves as a faculty residence and is not open to the public. The walk begins at the athletic compound centered on University Hall and moves to the academic campus, home of the three graduate professional schools.

University Hall

52. University Hall

Baskervill and Son with Anderson, Beckwith and Haible, 1960–1965

University Hall stands at the hub of the athletic complex on the North Grounds. Separated from the historic grounds and surrounded by parking, the building, capped by a scalloped dome, is a prominent landmark on the satellite campus. The startling size of the building is a commentary on the growth of the University and its athletic program in the post-World War II years. The ahistoric forms and detailing fall under the broad umbrella of the modern vocabularies that characterized University architecture between 1950 and the mid-1970s. Anderson, Beckwith, and Haible of Boston designed the new field house, completed in 1965. The structure's size, siting, and disregard for the past set the tone for the University's development of the North Grounds into the 1990s. Similar themes and rationales were repeated again and again as the satellite campus grew.

The new arena's precedents were far-flung rather than local. Unlike the architects of Memorial Gymnasium in the 1920s, the designers of the building, known locally as U Hall, did not look to the University's rich architectural tradition for inspiration. While a local reporter insisted that there was a connection, labeling the structure a "dried-up rotunda, shriveled after sucking a lemon," the designers cited economy and acoustics as the forces that determined the form. If the architects did not look to sources nearby, they did draw inspiration from contemporary work, such as Pier Luigi Nervi's Palazzo dello Sport for the 1960 Rome Olympics. Both buildings ultimately trace their lineage to Max Berg's 1912–13 reinforced concrete Jahrhunderthalle in Breslau.

The construction of University Hall was the latest in a series of transformations of the site on Copeley Hill during the twentieth century. The influx of veterans, taking advantage of the GI bill after World War II, and the later arrival of the "baby-boomers," fed the dramatic increase in the number of students—from fewer than 3,000 in 1940 to almost 10,000 in 1970. To house the swelling enrollments, the University purchased part of the former Massie dairy farm, which had been home to student boarders in the 1940s.

Upfitted with trailers and barracks, the rural site temporarily became a student housing compound. The construction of the arena less than twenty years later was yet another sweeping overhaul of the landscape.

The thirst for intercollegiate athletics underpinned the construction of University Hall. At the turn of the century, the rise of intercollegiate competition had sparked the creation of Lambeth Field and Fayerweather Gymnasium. Ongoing interest produced Memorial Gymnasium and Scott Stadium in the 1920s and 1930s. The University's controversial and hotly contested entry into the Atlantic Coast Conference in 1953 brought an additional pressure to provide suitable facilities for recruiting student athletes and for the drama of the spectacle. While Scott Stadium has been expanded with the addition of the upper decks, Memorial Gymnasium was spared a comparable overhaul. Instead, University Hall replaced it.

Although promoters of the project argued that the new arena was a mixed-use facility that could accommodate concerts as readily as athletic contests, the functions housed by the rest of the buildings in the complex suggest that sports were the dominant impulse. To the south, the Cage provides practice facilities, protected from the weather, for outdoor sports. Onesty Hall formerly contained a pool, prior to the opening of the Aquatic and Fitness Center. Practice fields and other athletic facilities cluster around. A sea of parking serves the compound and accommodates the form of transportation preferred by the spectators. Funded by alumni contributions and by allocations from the General Assembly, the building was not named to memorialize one of the University's athletic greats. Instead, the neutral name was chosen to reinforce the contention that the facility served all, not just the athletic slice, of the University community.

Continued growth of the athletic complex on Copeley Hill paralleled the growth of the campus. The McCue Center, also in a modern idiom, opened in 1991, to provide office, conference, and sports training spaces. Still, the additions have not kept pace with the mushrooming growth. With the admission of women, the demands of Title IX legislation, and the rising number of sports and students, the enormous facility is packed with activity. Talk of a replacement facility continues.

53. Klöckner Stadium   *VMDO, 1988–1992*

Klöckner Stadium, the most recent addition to the North Grounds athletic complex, caps the small rise and overlooks its ancestor below. Parking, already in place to serve U-Hall, supports the new facility. The name honors the principal donor, the neighboring Klöckner Group, a German-based conglomerate that had opened its first US plant in nearby Gordonsville. The University's successful soccer program formerly shared the facilities, includ-

Klöckner Stadium, 1988–1992, VMDO

ing an inhospitable artificial turf play-ing field, with other teams in Scott Stadium. Built primarily for a single sport, Klöckner Stadium contains an all-important natural turf field, pre-ferred by soccer teams. Local archi-tects VMDO conceived of the elegant minimalist design as a stadium within a park. The haunting silhouette stands out in bold relief against the woodland backdrop beyond. On the north, the bermed perimeter offers the viewer the option of informal grassy seating. The circular piers are not designed to accommodate future expansion. Instead, the piers and berm are skillful design devices used to define and sharpen the stadium edge.

54. Darden School   *Robert A. M. Stern with Ayers, Saint, Gross, 1992–1996*

The lavish Jeffersonian revival Darden School, by noted postmodernist Robert Stern, houses the University's graduate business program. The name honors Colgate Darden, the former University president who cam-paigned actively for the creation of the school. Opened in 1955, the gradu-ate school of business administration originally occupied Monroe Hall on the Central Grounds. In 1975, the Darden School joined the Law School and the Judge Advocate General's (JAG) School in the new graduate complex designed by Hugh Stubbins on the North Grounds. By 1996, the Darden School had sold its North Grounds building to the Law School and moved to more opulent quarters next door.

The style of the compound bypasses the Modernist idioms that dominated North Grounds architecture in the 1960 and 1970s, instead point-ing back to classical traditions of the Lawn. There is much of Jefferson in the new complex: the modular organization, the classical detailing, and the arrangement of the individual components to frame outdoor spaces are rem-iniscent of the Academical Village. Nonetheless, there are significant depar-tures. The expansive interior spaces, a dramatic departure from the colonial scale of the Jefferson buildings, are made possible by the use of modern materials. The Darden School's handsome greensward to the south is edged with smaller gardens, which are interwoven with a string of identical pavil-ions, all reminiscent of Pavilion IX on the Lawn. The animating variety and irregularity of the original Jefferson complex are tamed.

While the building's materials, massing, and detailing point directly to the architecture of the historic grounds, the planning does not.

Jefferson's Academical Village was intended to be a self-sufficient community. The early complex was more than an artfully arranged collection of buildings. It also included housing for the faculty and students, the professors' gardens, and an experimental farm. Stitched together by a system that brought water from neighboring hills, it was an organic compound whose tendrils trailed out into the landscape beyond. Despite the quotations from the past, the Darden School is a modern object in Jeffersonian dress, an imposing complex placed in a semi-rural setting and dependent on the automobile for only intermittent occupation. Behind the Jeffersonian bluster and gloss, lies the designers' attempt to marry the architectural vocabulary of the historic campus to the planning of the new.

If the planning of the Darden School is different from that of the Academical Village, it is typical of that of the North Grounds. The complex occupies a commanding position, sited at the crest of a small hill. Users come and go yet live elsewhere. The school fills the role of a suburban home, an imposing and isolated object, seen from a passing or approaching car. The expansive front parking lots characteristize the planning of the North Grounds generally, guided by automobile dependence. Unlike Jefferson's campus, the access is vehicular rather than pedestrian.

Despite the architectural quotations, the building's roots lie in the immediate, rather than a distant, past. The style not only embraces Jefferson but also rejects the school's Modernist quarters next door. While the state provided the school's two earlier homes, donors primarily funded this structure. The individual pieces of the building, named to honor these contributors, document this financial history. In size and detailing, the complex is an academical village for a single school, a Jeffersonesque compound, dropped onto a suburban campus.

Darden School, 1992–1996, Robert A. M. Stern with Ayers, Saint, Gross

55. School of Law and Judge Advocate
General's School

School of Law

Hugh Stubbins & Associates with Stainback and Scribner, 1968–1974; Ayers, Saint, Gross, 1994–1997

Judge Advocate General's School

Hugh Stubbins & Associates with Rawlings, Wilson and Fraher, 1968–1975

The Law School, one of Jefferson's original schools, had occupied a series of prominent homes on the campus, including Pavilion III, Pavilion X, the Rotunda basement, Minor Hall, and Clark Hall. It became one of the first academic programs to leave the main grounds. The JAG School, housed nearby when the Law School resided in Clark Hall, joined the move to the north. The Darden School now occupies new quarters next door.

The School of Law today occupies two buildings of the 1970s complex designed by Hugh Stubbins and Associates. The former Darden School building is on the west. The Law School originally occupied only the east wing of the present structure. Two new wings, designed by Ayers, Saint, Gross of Baltimore and completed in 1997, knit together the two separate buildings to form a quadrangle around an interior courtyard. The Judge Advocate General's School remains in the Stubbins-designed building next door.

Like McKim, Mead & White nearly three-quarters of a century before, the 1960s designers of the professional compound on the North Grounds adapted the Jefferson vocabulary to changing systems of taste. Where McKim, Mead & White and their successors had inflated the local idiom to suit their grand cultural aspirations, Hugh Stubbins and Associates distilled and abstracted Jefferson's work to produce buildings for the suburban University. The planning of the academic compound on the North Grounds is typical of the period: buildings line the road, and are tightly

School of Law, 1968–1975, Hugh Stubbins and Associates with Stainback and Scribner. School of Law addition, including new entrance wing, 1994–1997, Ayers Saint Gross

bound to their parking. The asymmetry, the pronounced horizontal composition reinforced by layering crisply cut bands of the planar wall surface, the lack of historical ornament, and the impression of horizontal floating volumes were hallmarks of Modern design. Still, red brick and white trim—although in this case, a concrete frame with brick and concrete infill panels—echo the local paradigm. The buildings also indicate the darker dimension latent in the Modernist palette: the commitment to minimalism danced uneasily on the edge of banalism as the University struggled to house rapidly swelling enrollments and expanding programs on a shrinking budget. Both lofty aesthetic ambitions and practical financial considerations affected the design of Stubbins's subsequent much-maligned complex.

Relocating the three professional schools to a compound on the North Grounds marked a highly controversial step. Several reasons guided the selection of the three schools. Each was essentially a self-sufficient program and had also outgrown its facilities on the Central Grounds. The North Grounds sites were also conveniently near the married student housing on Copeley Hill. Promoters argued that the new facilities, developed from scratch on a new site, could be molded to accommodate specialized educational needs and hefty parking requirements. Others, however, regretted the move from the collegial atmosphere and the loss of the school's historic home on the Central Grounds.

Continued growth and changes in taste have transformed the academic facilities on the North Grounds. An addition to the JAG school was completed in 1991 by Bohlin, Powell, Larkin, Cywinski, a noted contemporary firm, in collaboration with Johnson, Craven and Gibson. In 1996, when the Darden School moved to its neo-Jeffersonian palace next door, the Law School purchased the abandoned quarters, now named Slaughter Hall. Ayers, Saint, Gross of Baltimore renovated and expanded the two buildings. The handsome cherry-paneled reading room, a skillful insert into a former bleak interior courtyard, is worth a visit. The new entry is a clever conflation of allusions to earlier architecture. The neo-modernized classicism of the entrance is a suitable reference to the stripped planar style of federal architecture in the 1930s, often used for courthouses. The standing seam metal roof and cupola over the Caplin Pavilion nod to Jefferson. At the same time, the overall composition points directly to the law school's prior homes—to Clark Hall and through Clark Hall, ultimately to Minor Hall. The organization of the Law School facade is hauntingly familiar—a three-part composition with a recessed central entry behind a trabeated screen, capped by a pyramidal roof. With great restraint, the design distills the facades of the school's historic homes into a minimal design of abstract planes. The inscription above the doors, a duplicate of the one from the frieze of Clark Hall, is another echo from the school's memory. The entry is a symbol that builds a bridge to the Law School's past and attempts to reinterpret Jefferson and his successors, yet again, in light of contemporary tastes.

Observatory Mountain

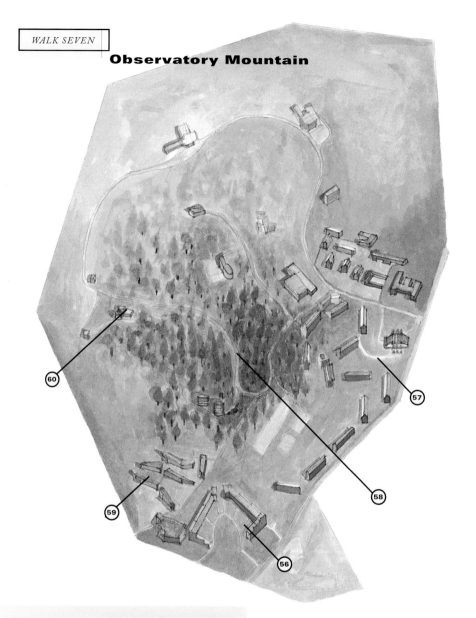

56 | Gooch-Dillard Residences
57 | Alderman Road Residences and
   | Observatory Dining Hall
58 | University Water System and Reservoir
59 | Hereford College
60 | Leander McCormick Observatory

The Occupation of Observatory Hill

Observatory Mountain dominated one of two non-contiguous parcels that formed the original land holdings of the University. The Academical Village became the pampered centerpiece of the easternmost tract. The mountain site, to the west, played the supporting role. It provided water, wood, and stone for the academic community, and Jefferson dreamed of an observatory at its crown. These early intentions guided the spotty development of the mountain throughout the nineteenth century. The Old Reservoir was a fruit of the relentless quest to secure an adequate water supply for the Academical Village. The McCormick Observatory, built long after the Jefferson period, finally fulfilled his dream. The overlay of medieval details on the building, safely removed from the Academical Village and dedicated to scientific study, captures the nineteenth-century reverence for and ambivalence toward the rise of science.

The University's eventual occupation of the mountain, later called Observatory Hill, came only after the middle of the twentieth century. By then, Observatory Road, now McCormick Road, had developed as the University's science complex. The spillover from that precinct, including structures such as the nuclear reactor, now dots Observatory Hill. Nearby, a series of student housing projects, molded by the concerns of the Suburban Campus period, march toward the summit. A recent addition is Robert Stern's delightful annex to a 1970s dining facility, a jewel that is at the heart of the recent Jefferson revival on the grounds.

56. Gooch-Dillard Residences

Edward Larrabee Barnes Associates, 1980–1984

The Gooch-Dillard residences provided much-needed housing for the rapidly expanding student population in the 1980s. Between 1970 and 1985 the University enrollment grew from just under 10,000 to over 17,000. To accommodate this dizzying growth, University officials confronted a host of challenges that ranged from empirical to social and psychological. Their concerns centered not only on quantity—how to house an unprecedented number of people and where to locate the dormitories on the crowded grounds—but also quality of life—how to use the architecture to counter the sense of alienation and anonymity as the Academical Village expanded to the size of a small city. The Gooch-Dillard complex represented an alternative to a much larger student housing project on the Birdwood tract failed to materialize.

Purchased in 1967, the Birdwood tract was originally seen as the solution to the housing crisis. President Shannon described the 550-acre parcel as "the last, large, undeveloped area anywhere near the university." By 1971, the University had designated the site for student housing and had proposed to build a bridge over the Route 250 Bypass to connect the remote tract to the rest of the University. Preliminary plans called for six residential colleges to house 3,000 students by 1980. The residential college, with students and faculty living together, was envisioned as a modern recapitulation of the Academical Village. By 1980, the notion of a satellite campus at Birdwood was dead—abandoned as too expensive. Instead, a golf course, which replaced the links lost with the construction of the McCormick Road residences at mid-century, opened in the 1980s.

Compared with the vast complex originally planned for Birdwood, the Gooch-Dillard dormitories represented a more modest proposal for student housing nearer the Central Grounds. Designed in the early 1980s, they are formally a transitional project: neither motel modern, like the Alderman Road dormitories next door, nor neo-Jeffersonian, like the nearby contemporary addition to the Observatory Hill Dining Hall. The red brick and white trim at the Gooch-Dillard housing nods to the local idiom. The outdoor covered and colonnaded walkways are also faintly reminiscent of Jefferson's work. Nonetheless, the sharp, blocky, prismatic massing and lack of historicizing ornament are purely Modern. The project's sensitive siting, wrapped around a shallow ravine and set beneath the woodland cover, is typical of the work of the architect, Edward Larrabee Barnes. The building names honor noted Professor of Political Science Robert K. Gooch and former dean of the Law School Hardy C. Dillard. Continued University growth has forced the construction of additional dormitory space nearby. Subsequently, the Gooch-Dillard residences were incorporated as one edge of the Hereford College complex beyond, as the ever expanding University placed even more student housing on Observatory Hill.

57. Alderman Road Residences and Observatory Dining Hall

Alderman Road Residences   *Johnson, Craven and Gibson, 1962–1967*
Observatory Hill Dining Hall   *Williams and Tazewell, 1972–1974; Robert A. M. Stern*
with Marcellus Wright, Cox and Smith, 1983–1984

Although the vast McCormick Road dormitory project, completed in the early 1950s, anticipated the future growth of the University, by the early 1960s, even more space was needed. The Alderman Road residences, designed by local architects Johnson, Craven, and Gibson, opened in two phases, in 1964 and 1967. The style, placement, and planning link these structures to other University projects of the period. Removed from the Academical Village, the buildings occupy a formerly wooded site near the earlier McCormick Road Residences. Unlike the earlier dormitories across the road, which were sited to frame outdoor rooms, the long, rectangular buildings that make up the Alderman Road residences are clustered informally or casually scattered along the edge of the site. In their placement, the individual objects were unrelated to each other and to the whole. The style, too, was radically different from that of the earlier student housing: exposed structural frames and hovering volumes replaced the brick, neo-Georgian forms seen as appropriate ten years earlier.

Near the intersection of Alderman and McCormick Roads is the original Observatory Hill Dining Hall, completed in 1974. The controversial building replaced a cafeteria on the Central Grounds in Newcomb Hall with a new facility adjacent to the 1960s dorms. University officials sited the

McCormick Road Residences (page 90)

Observatory Hill Dining Hall, 1972–1974, Williams and Tazewell. Observatory Hill Dining Hall addition, 1983–1984, Robert A. M. Stern with Marcellus Wright, Cox and Smith

dining hall near the dormitories to promote a "residential college atmosphere" for the "ever-expanding university." The undistinguished brick "shed roof modern" structure, like the Alderman Road dormitories, displayed another modernist formula that became the norm during the Campus Suburban period between 1950 and the mid-1970s.

By contrast, the elegant 1984 addition to the dining hall references the traditional architecture of the Grounds. Robert A. M. Stern was among a number of high-profile architects promoted by the former architecture school dean, Jaquelin Robertson, to redirect the design of the University's architecture. Stern's neo-Jeffersonian work became one of the first. The handsome porches on the north and south of the existing dining hall reference the traditional architecture of the grounds. The brick arcade, the Tuscan columns, and pyramidal roofed pavilions rework familiar local themes. However, the references depart from the model. Stern's Tuscan order is drawn from Werner Hegemann and Elbert Peets's *American Vitruvius*, rather than from Jefferson's milk-bottle shaped columns on the Lawn. The brick arches are low and segmental in contrast to the semicircular arches found on the Ranges. The paired columns frame individual, contiguous pavilions. There are no intermediate colonnades. The roof, a file of pyramidal caps, each topped by a square cupola, is unprecedented in Jefferson's work. The expanses of glazing create a Modernist's dream: light-filled interiors by day, with the facade a string of glowing lanterns by night. The detailing of the steel sash to form smaller panes is modern and traditional; the file of pavilions set in the lacy landscape is deferential and arresting. Despite the awkward connection between old and new, the twin four-bay porches, out of the tradition of grand dining halls, transform the act of everyday student dining into a festive communal event.

58. University Water System and Reservoir

University Water System   *1819–present*
Reservoir   *Major Green Peyton, 1867–1869*

Securing an adequate water supply concerned the University founders and remained a perennial problem for administrators into the twentieth century. A shortage of funding led to spotty and piecemeal construction, plaguing development. Jefferson arranged the construction of a pipeline of hollowed logs from springs on Observatory Mountain to the Academical Village in 1819–20. The impermanent system soon required additional attention. By the 1830s, a scattered patchwork of cisterns, to collect roof runoff, and wells dotted the grounds. These supplemented the water piped in from further away. Eventually iron pipes replaced the wooden lines. Despite the fact that the site of the Academical Village drained well, inadequate provisions for waste removal created health problems.

As the University grew during the nineteenth century, so did its water needs. In 1853–54, the General Assembly appropriated funds to rework the system. The relative paucity of the allocation and immensity of the problem produced delays. The University hired Charles Ellet, one of the great civil engineers of the period, to prepare a comprehensive plan. Following Ellet's recommendation, the University installed new iron pipelines to carry the water from the west to a reservoir located near the site later occupied by the chapel. A steam pump forced the water to a pair of 7,000-gallon storage tanks at the base of the Rotunda dome. From this elevated position, water was gravity-fed to the University's buildings. However, the solution to this one problem created another. Leaks from the containers damaged both the books and the building. Nonetheless, the tanks remained in operation until the 1880s.

In order to bypass the unsatisfactory tanks, the Board of Visitors continued to press for another alternative. In 1867, it authorized the construction of a dam to create a reservoir on Observatory Mountain. Completed in 1869 by Major Green Peyton, an engineer and the future proctor, the reservoir finally satiated, at least temporarily, the water needs. The reservoir, no longer a source of water for the University and until recently used as cooling pond for the nuclear reactor, is a fragment of this nineteenth-century system.

By the 1880s, the water situation was again desperate. In 1884–85, the University entered into a joint venture with Charlottesville to construct a new "water works." The Ragged Mountain Reservoir and water mains supplied both the city and the University. The city built its first filtration plant about 1922, on University property, near the site of the present Observatory Mountain plant. Water storage tanks nearer the top of the hill were added in the early 1970s. Water from the Ragged Mountain Reservoir, processed through the Observatory Mountain Treatment Plant, remains the primary source for the University system today.

59. Hereford College

Tod Williams, Billie Tsein and Associates with VMDO, 1990–1992

The designers of Hereford College deconstructed and then reconstructed Jefferson's original composition for the Academical Village to meet the challenges of the expanding University in the late twentieth century. Designed by Tod Williams, Billie Tsein and Associates, the complex, originally known as the New College, was renamed in 1994 to honor the University's fifth President, Frank L. Hereford Jr. Five finger-like dormitories step down the steep slope, from the principal's house at the crest to the dining facility at the base. Together with the existing Gooch-Dillard dormitories to the east, the buildings form the perforated edge of an irregular green space, carved from the wooded site on Observatory Hill. The abstract composition of buildings, draped across the sloping site to frame views of the landscape beyond, draws on a rich assortment of historic models.

Like its predecessor, Brown College, Hereford College is a residential college. University officials saw the residential-college form as a twenti-

Hereford College

eth-century recasting of Jefferson's Academical Village. Like the professors of the Academical Village, the college principal, a University faculty member, lives near the students. Similar to the early Academical Village, Hereford College is a somewhat self-sufficient community. It includes not only living quarters but also facilities for dining, meeting, and such twentieth-century needs as computer labs and laundry equipment. American residential colleges loosely mimic their English counterparts. Like other American residential colleges but unlike the English, Hereford College's communal events focus on extracurricular activities rather than on academic instruction. Within the enlarged University, residential colleges form sets of smaller communities to re-create the vitality natural to an institution of more compact size. The desire to foster and enhance a sense of community is built into the structure of the architecture. The large dining hall, the green space, and the stairs, which, as in Alvar Aalto's work, double as amphitheater seating, offer the inhabitants a variety of opportunities for gathering and interaction.

There is much of Jefferson in the design of Hereford College. The use of brick as the dominant material and the arrangement of the buildings to frame a large greensward make direct references to the Lawn. At the new college, neatly geometric terraces, like those of the Lawn, regularize the sixty-foot drop from the principal's house to the dining hall. The focal points of both complexes are key buildings that embody and house the driving intentions behind the whole. Jefferson's library was the most important building of the Lawn. The analogue at Hereford College is the building for community gatherings at the base of the complex, a glazed structure with a taut steel portico. Like Jefferson, the twentieth-century designers molded, manipulated, and deformed the preliminary layout to accommodate the topography.

Despite the similarities, Hereford College transforms Jeffersonian design principles, filtering them through twentieth-century Modernism and Deconstructionism. Where Jefferson's complex displayed a serene, rational, idealized vision, overlaid on the landscape, Hereford College is intentionally fragmented and incomplete. The long court focuses on a pair of buildings, the faceted principal's residence to the north and the glazed Runk Dining Hall to the south. Unlike the Rotunda, both are pointedly off axis. At Hereford College, no colonnades measure the rhythm of the processional down the site. Instead, one moves through, not alongside, the pavilion-like termini of the long dormitory buildings. The architectural vocabulary is assertively Modern and reminiscent of Dutch housing projects of the 1920s and 1930s. The planar walls, unembellished openings, flat roofs, corner windows, and steel sash—pointedly not painted white—distance the project from its classically inspired ancestor. Unlike the nearly contemporary Darden School, the references to Jefferson are oblique rather than literal. Shunning the opportunity for direct quotation, the designers of Hereford College sought instead a conflation of modernity and historic precedent.

60. Leander McCormick Observatory *1881–1885*

McCormick Observatory composes one link in a chain of University structures dedicated to astronomical study. Jefferson's interest in astronomy left a number of marks on the University. Astronomy was included in his original curriculum as part of the school of natural philosophy. He suggested that the dome of the Rotunda be upfitted as a planetarium by painting the interior of the dome blue and covering it with gilt stars to replicate the patterns of the heavens. Without the funds for a new structure, he reconsidered reworking the Monroe Hill house as an observatory. He also prepared a plan for an observatory c. 1825 and visited the site proposed for an observatory on the crest of a small mountain west of the grounds, which became known as Observatory Hill. A structure, called an observatory and perhaps based on a Jefferson design, was built on the site in 1828. Lacking the appropriate equipment for astronomical use, the building was demolished in 1859. According to a local legend, William Pratt, first superintendent of buildings and grounds at the University, oversaw the demolition and reused the stone to build his now vanished Gothic Revival gatekeeper's cottage, near the site of Alderman Library. Around 1900, following construction of the McCormick Observatory, a small students' observatory appeared near Dawson's Row.

During the nineteenth century, support for an astronomy program at the University grew. In 1866, the Board of Visitors contemplated the creation of a separate school of astronomy, to be headed by Matthew Fontaine Maury. Lack of funding ended the plans. In 1878, Leander J. McCormick, a brother of Cyrus McCormick, offered the University one of the largest telescopes in the world and provided the funds for a structure to house it. The Clark telescope, donated by McCormick, is still inside. William H. Vanderbilt and a group of alumni and friends of the University endowed the chair, which was required for the McCormick bequest. Professor Ormand Stone was named the first director of the observatory in 1882.

The site and the building, which housed the state-of-the-art equipment, are layered with rich associations to the past. The plans for an observatory on the mountain go back to the moment of the founding of the University. The construction of the McCormick Observatory picked up this dropped thread. Built on the site of the previous observatory, which had been demolished 25 years earlier, it formed a link between old and new. As originally built, the structure included the dome room and the two-bay workspace to the north. Like the nearly contemporary University chapel, the observatory also displays medieval motifs but on a building with an entirely different function. The observatory's medieval detailing, the heavy stepped buttresses, and the recessed round-arched windows dignified a building dedicated to science. Warner and Swasey of Cleveland, Ohio, designed the structure's revolving hemispherical dome and the mechanical system,

Leander McCormick Observatory

which was originally manually operated. Building another bridge to the past, Stone suggested that the hill be renamed Mount Jefferson, to commemorate the crucial role that the founder played in the establishment of the University's observatory.

The sophisticated structure, funded by McCormick, remained the University's main observatory until the construction of the Fan Mountain Observatory in the 1970s. By then, the lights and haze of Charlottesville and the development of new technologies necessitated another facility. Although the McCormick Observatory remains a living science research center, it is most significant today as a belated fruit of a Jefferson plan and for the rare operating late-nineteenth-century telescope within.

Bibliography

Collections

Facilities Management Resource Center
Law School Archives
Special Collections Department, University of Virginia Library

University of Virginia Periodicals

Alumni Bulletin of the University of Virginia
Cavalier Daily
College Topics
Colonnade: The News Journal of the School of Architecture, University of Virginia
Corks and Curls
University Journal
University of Virginia *Alumni News*
University of Virginia Magazine
Virginia Law Weekly
Virginia Spectator

Books and Articles

Abernethy, Thomas Perkins. *Historical Sketch of the University of Virginia*. Richmond: Dietz Press, 1948.

Adams, Herbert Baxter. *Thomas Jefferson and the University of Virginia*. U. S. Bureau of Education, Circular of Information no.1. Washington, D.C.: GPO, 1888.

Adams, William Howard, ed. *The Eye of Thomas Jefferson*. Charlottesville: University Press of Virginia, 1981.

Barringer, Anna. "Pleasant It Is to Remember These Things." *Magazine of Albemarle County History* 24 (1965–1966): 5–38, 27–28 (1968–1969, 1970): 5–116.

Barringer, Paul Brandon, James Mercer Garnett, and Rosewell Page. *University of Virginia*. 2 vols. New York: Lewis Publishing Company, 1904.

Bruce, Philip Alexander. *History of the University of Virginia, 1819–1919*. 5 vols. New York: Macmillan, 1920–1922.

Clemons, Harry. *The University of Virginia Library, 1825–1950*. Charlottesville: University of Virginia Library, 1954.

Culbreth, David M. R. *The University of Virginia: Memories of Her Student-Life and Professors*. New York and Washington, D.C.: Neale Publishing Co., 1908.

Dabney, Virginius. *Mr. Jefferson's University*. Charlottesville: University Press of Virginia, 1981.

Dashiell III, David A. "Between Earthly Wisdom and Heavenly Truth: The Effort to Build a Chapel at the University of Virginia, 1835–1890." M.A. thesis, University of Virginia, 1992.

Dennis, Michael. "Reforming the 'Academical Village': Edwin A. Alderman and the University of Virginia, 1904–1915." *Virginia Magazine of History and Biography* 105: 1 (Winter 1997): 53–86.

Eddins, Joe. *Around the Corner after World War I*. Charlottesville: Published by the author, 1973.

Grizzard, Frank. "Documentary History of the Construction of the Buildings at the University of Virginia, 1817–1828." Ph.D. diss., University of Virginia, 1996.

Hantman, Jeffrey L. *Brooks Hall at the University of Virginia: Unravelling the Mystery.* (http://minerva.acc.virginia.edu/~anthro/Brooks.history/jh–bh1.html).

Hogan, Pendleton. *The Lawn: A Guide to Jefferson's University.* Charlottesville: University Press of Virginia, 1987.

Jefferson, Thomas. *Notes on the State of Virginia.* 1787. Ed. William H. Peden. Chapel Hill: University of North Carolina Press, 1954.

Kimball, Fiske. *Thomas Jefferson, Architect.* 1916. With a new introduction by Frederick D. Nichols. New York: DaCapo Press, 1968.

Lambeth, William Alexander, and Warren Henry Manning. *Thomas Jefferson as an Architect and Designer of Landscapes.* Boston: Houghton Mifflin, 1913.

Lasala, Joseph Michael. "Thomas Jefferson's Designs for the University of Virginia." M.A. thesis, University of Virginia, 1992.

Lay, K. Edward. "Charlottesville's Architectural Legacy." *Magazine of Albemarle County History* 46 (May 1988): 28–95.

McHugh, Kevin. "Form and Fitness: John Rochester Thomas and Brooks Museum at the University of Virginia." M.A. thesis, University of Virginia, 1987.

Malone, Dumas. *Jefferson and His Time.* 6 vols. Boston: Little, Brown, 1948–1981.

————. *Edwin A. Alderman: A Biography.* New York: Doubleday, Doran and Company, 1940.

Matthews, Sarah S. *The University of Virginia Hospital (Its First Fifty Years).* Charlottesville: The Michie Company, 1960.

Moore, John Hammond. *Albemarle: Jefferson's County, 1727–1976.* Charlottesville: University Press of Virginia, 1976.

Nichols, Frederick Doveton. "A Day to Remember: The Burning of the Rotunda, 1895." *Magazine of Albemarle County History* 17 (1958–59): 57–65.

————. *Thomas Jefferson's Architectural Drawings.* 1960. 4th ed. Charlottesville: Thomas Jefferson Memorial Foundation, 1978.

————and Ralph E. Griswold. *Thomas Jefferson: Landscape Architect.* Charlottesville: University Press of Virginia, 1978.

O'Neal, William B. *Jefferson's Buildings at the University of Virginia: The Rotunda.* Charlottesville: The University of Virginia Press, 1960.

————. *Jefferson's Fine Arts Library: His Selections for the University of Virginia, Together with His Own Architectural Books.* Charlottesville: University Press of Virginia, 1976.

————. "Michele and Giacomo Raggi at the University of Virginia: With Notes and Documents." *Magazine of Albemarle County History* 18 (1959–1960): 5–32.

————. *Pictorial History of the University of Virginia.* 2nd ed. Charlottesville: University Press of Virginia, 1980.

————. "The Workmen at the University of Virginia, 1817–1826: With Notes and Documents." *Magazine of Albemarle County History* 17 (1958–1959): 5–48.

Pavilion I, University of Virginia: Historic Structure Report. Albany, NY: Mendel, Mesick, Cohen, Waite, Hall Architects, 1988.

Pavilion II, University of Virginia: Historic Structure Report. Albany, NY: Mesick, Cohen, Waite Architects, 1992.

Pavilion V, University of Virginia: Historic Structure Report. Albany, NY: Mesick, Cohen, Waite Architects, 1994.

Pavilion VI, University of Virginia: Historic Structure Report. Albany, NY: Mesick, Cohen, Waite Architects, 1991.

Patton, John S., and Sallie J. Doswell. *The University of Virginia: Glimpses of Its Past and Present.* Lynchburg, VA: J. P. Bell Company, 1900.

Ritchie, John. *The First Hundred Years: A Short History of the School of Law of the University of Virginia for the Period 1826–1926.* Charlottesville: University Press of Virginia, 1978.

Shawen, Neil McDowell. "The Casting of a Lengthened Shadow: Thomas Jefferson's Role in Determining the Site for a State University in Virginia." Ph.D. diss., George Washington University, 1980.

Shenkir, William G. and William R. Wilkerson. *University of Virginia's McIntire School of Commerce: The First Seventy-Five Years, 1921–1996*. Charlottesville: McIntire School of Commerce Foundation, 1996.

Tarter, Brent. "The Making of a University President: John Lloyd Newcomb and the University of Virginia, 1931–1933." *Virginia Magazine of History and Biography* 87: 4 (Oct 1979): 474–481.

Trimble, Marsha. "The Legacy of Clark Hall." *UVA Lawyer* 21:3 (Fall 1997): 41–47.

Turner, Paul Venable. *Campus: An American Planning Tradition*. Cambridge: MIT Press, 1984.

Vaughan, Joseph Lee, and Omer Allan Gianniny. *Thomas Jefferson's Rotunda Restored*. Charlottesville: University Press of Virginia, 1981.

Wells, John E. and Robert E. Dalton. *The Virginia Architects, 1835–1955: A Biographical Dictionary*. Richmond, VA: New South Architectural Press, 1997.

Wilkerson, William R. and William G. Shenkir. *Paul G. McIntire: Businessman and Philanthropist*. Charlottesville: McIntire School of Commerce Foundation, 1988.

Williams, Dorothy Hunt. *Historic Virginia Gardens*. Charlottesville: Published for the Garden Club of Virginia by the University Press of Virginia, 1975.

Wilson, Richard Guy. *"Arise and Build!" A Centennial Commemoration of the 1895 Rotunda Fire*. Charlottesville: University of Virginia Library, 1995.

———, ed. *Thomas Jefferson's Academical Village: The Creation of an Architectural Masterpiece*. Charlottesville: Bayly Art Museum of the University of Virginia, 1993.

———, ed. *The Architecture of Thomas Jefferson*. (http://jefferson.village.virginia.edu/wilson/)

Yetter, George Humphrey. "Stanford White at the University of Virginia: The New Buildings on the South Lawn and the Reconstruction of the Rotunda in 1896." M.A. thesis, University of Virginia, 1980.

———. "Stanford White at the University of Virginia: Some New Light on an Old Question." *Journal of the Society of Architectural Historians* 40 (Dec 1981): 320–325.

Illustration Credits

Index